Windows 7

I0502913

This training manual is designed to explain to you the functions of Windows 7,

This manual is also suitable for people who have never worked on a computer before.

This manual will help you prepare for the SAQA exam's

Unit standard 117867.116932,117902/258883 Operating a personal Computer

Computer Awareness   Module 1
- Understand what computer hardware devices are
- Understand what software programs are
- Understand what an Operating system is
- Understand what Windows 7 is

Desktop fundementals   Module 2
- What is Shortcut icons
- Moving shortcut icons
- Deleting shortcuts
- What is the start menu
- Pinning programs to the start menu
- Creating a short cut to the desktop
- What is the taskbar
- Pinning programs to the taskbar

Exploring windows   Module 3
- What is a window
- Moving a window
- Resizing a window
- Minimizing, Maximizing and Closing windows
- Cascading windows
- Stacking windows

Managing files and folders   Module 4
- What is Windows Explorer
- Browsing folders
- Browsing files
- Creating folders
- Creating subfolders
- Filtering files
- Searching for data
- Moving, copying and deleting files
- Creating libraries

Control panel   Module 5
- Power options
- Backup and Restore
- Firewall
- Using internet via Bluetooth
- Adding printers
- Installing and uninstalling programs
- What to do if your computer doesn't work
- Screen saver
- Changing desktop background
- Changing the mouse settings
- Changing currency, date and time
- Sound settings
- User accounts
- Parental control
- Speech recognition

About this manual

This training manual is designed to explain to you the functions of Windows 7,
This manual is also suitable for people who have never worked on a computer before.

The following are used <> to indicate to either type in a word or select a menu item, at no point must you type in <> especialy not when your saving files.

➤ This icon ,the arrow key in front of this line, indicates a list of instructions to follow

⌐ The preceding icon is indicative of optional instructions

At times you wil find red circles and arrows that indicate where you must click

There are practical exercises that is recommended for your to complete during each module.

There is an estimated time period in which you could complete the modules however you could be able to complete it in a shorter time or you could take a little bit longer. Each person are unique and have there own pace to work on.. It is recommended that you do some more exercises after the first day of training.

There is also additional exercises at the end of this manual that you can complete at your own perusal or on the instructions of your trainer. Do as many exercises until you feel comfortable.

You can go to any training organization that have acredited evaluators to evaluate you, and give you credits for exam 116932,117902/258883 after they found you competent in theory and pracise of this training material.

Exam 116932,117902/258883 is the current unit standard in south africa for using a GUI operating system
Exam 117867 test your knowledge on managing files within a GUI operating system environment

The unit standard for above information may differ in your country.

After completing this training material you will be able to master the contents of above information and pass any exam that will be testing above information.

Should you wish to order more training material please

Send any queries to Email: Quality1Training@gmail.com

Yolandie Mostert have trained thousands of students in spreadsheet programs, word programs and windows programs. She will enjoy training you. However the manuals are well explained and therefor you can train yourself with this training material, without a tutor.

Any other training material can be designed for you on request, please send an email, if you want any other training material. Microsoft word and Microsoft excel training material is also available.

This training manual is designed by Yolandie Mostert copyright©2014

No copies are allowed without written permission

Computer Awareness   Module 1

Estimated time 60 min

After completion of this module you will be able to:

        Understand what computer hardware devices are
        Understand what software programs are
        Understand what an Operating system is
        Understand what a Windows program is

Computer Hardware devices
The computer (Hardware)
The following are identified to be computer hardware

Input device:

The Mouse

The mouse is a device you use to interact with the computer, certain functions are being activated by clicking with the mouse. The mouse is called an input device because you use the mouse to access information on your pc. *Thus the computer receive programming instructions(input) from the mouse*

Different type of mice
There are different types of mice available for the computer and none of them byte!
Although in this course you will be introduced to "bits and bytes" that is not dangerous at all.
There are wireless mice and also mice that gets connected to your computer via USB port or PS2.
The older computers are mostly connected via PS2 and the newer computers connect via USB.
Before you purchase a mouse, make sure what connections is available on your computer.

How to operate the mouse:
Position the mouse on any flat spaced area, usually on the desktop area next to the computer. There are mouse pads available *that provides a smooth working area*. When you move the mouse up, right left or down, there will be a cursor, usually an arrow key that will move on the screen in the direction you move the mouse. Sometimes the cursor changes shape for different functions in different programs.

The left button
You use the mouse by clicking to activate certain parts of a software program. On the mouse, there are two buttons, the left, and the right button. In most programs, you press the Left mouse button to activate certain parts of a software program and to select certain data in a program, you will hold down the left mouse button.

The right mouse button
The right mouse button is used to activate special shortcut menus for that specific program.

Dragging
In this course we will refer to the word "Dragging" which indicates that you must click with the left mouse button and not Release the mouse button and then move the mouse up down, right or left, according to the instructions. Usually in a program, this will select that specific area, so that you can apply certain functions to the selected data. "
Earlier versions of computer programs did not operate with a mouse, users had to operate programs only with a keyboard.

The Keyboard

The keyboard is called an input device, since you input data via the keyboard into the computer. The Keyboard is a flat plate, electronic board with alphabetic characters and numbers on it. You use the keyboard to type letters or numbers into a document. When you press a character on the keyboard it can appear on the screen if you're working in, for example, a word processing program.

There are also special function keys on the keyboard that you will learn later when you start working on different programs. Each function key has specific actions in different programs.

There are different keyboards available and some of the alphabetical characters are located on different places on different keyboards. In America and South Africa most people use the QWERTY keyboard, and many French people in Europe use the AZERTY keyboard, though some Europeans also use the QWERTY keyboard. You can ask the shop assistant which keyboard you desire. You can find the QWERTY keyboard easily by looking at the top line of the alphabet characters, on the left side, the first character should be Q, the next one W, E,R,T,Y.

Liquid and food stuff should not be placed close to the keyboard since it is difficult to remove food Particles from the keyboard. *The functions of the keyboard are explained in detail at the end of this module.*

Output device:
Computer screen (Monitor)

The monitor is where you view programs and data. In computer terms it is identified to be an output device. The monitor has its own power on/off switch that needs to be switched on/off and sometimes has its own power cable. Today all monitors are in colour, older monitors are in black And white or S/VGA which is a different quality colour screen.

Printer

Printers are called output devices because you print the data out on a piece of paper. There are many different type of printers, dot matrix, desk jet and laser printers. Small Dot matrix printers are the cheapest and thus have the lowest quality however they print very slowly..

Deskjet printers are more expensive and can print in colour and black and white. Prices range from R300 up to R1000 for desk jet colour printers. Small business owners usually purchase Desktop printers. They are fast enough and do not cost that much and produce good quality print outs. Laser printers are high quality printers and can be very expensive. IT range anything from R1200 .Laser printers are very fast, and thus you can print many documents fast. It is more important to know what the cost of the printer cartridge is, before purchasing a printer, since some ink cartridges are less expensive than others, and thus you will be saving money when you purchase a printer that use in expensive cartridges.

Inside the Computer Box:
The BOX /CPU/Computer/Case

The box next to the screen is identified to be the computer sometimes also called the CPU. The reason for this is because inside the Box you will find one of the most important devices which is called the CPU (Central Processing Unit).The CPU is connected to the main-board also called the motherboard.

The motherboard/Mainboard

Is the largest electronic board located inside the box (case). All the smaller units are connected to this board. There are many different type of motherboards just like cars, some are faster, some slower and some have nifty functions which you never use.

Fitted onto the motherboard is the CPU and RAM (Random Access Memory)

You can buy extra RAM chips and have them fitted if the motherboards capacity allows it.

RAM (Random Access Memory)
This is the temporary storage area of the computer. Whatever you see on the screen is programs/data that are loaded into temporary storage on your computer.
This means if there is a power failure, your data will be lost and cannot be recovered.
This is why it is important for you to store data to a permanent storage area.

BIOS (Basic Input Output System)
The BIOS is a little hardwired program that starts your computer and do fault finding, and loads your Operating System into RAM. It is possible to change some of the settings on your BIOS, however this is not advisable and not recommendable during the introduction course.
Warning: do not make changes to the BIOS, if you are not familiar with the processes.

CPU (Central Processing Unit)
The CPU is like the manager of all the hardware devices, it controls all the processing and allocates resources to priority tasks. The CPU communicates with the software program called the "Operating system", that is permanently loaded on the hard disk.

Storage devices
The hard disk   is also called the C:\ drive [C:\ referred to as the Root directory]
This is the Permanent Storage area where data is stored via the RAM
The hard disk is a round disk divided into tracks and sectors and is located inside the computer box, and connected to the motherboard.
Data and programs are permanently stored on the C: drive for quick easy access.
On earlier computers there was no hard disk and data and programs had to be loaded onto the RAM.
Other storage devices:
A:\drive
The capacity of the stiffy is 1.44 MB. Many new computers is not designed with a stiffy drive
Data stored on stiffy are not very reliable and has limited storage capacity.
CD
Data and programs can be stored on CD
CD's are more reliable and have much more storage capacity
USB
USB is the most recommendable storage option, since it has a large storage capacity
And is easy to transport. This medium is very reliable.
Network/Internet
Data can also be stored on the network or internet
Hard disk partitioning
Although you can connect more than one hard disk onto your computer, you can also divide one hard disk into 2 pieces, which is called hard disk partitioning.
When you partition a hard disk and create two partitions, it will appear to you that the one hard disk now have two different drives. For example if you only had a C drive, you can partition that drive that it will appear and function as if you have a C, and a D drive , when you create two partitions.
Thus it will look and function like you have 2 hard disks, however in reality it is only 1 disk that has been partitioned.

Naming of storage devices
The storage devices are named in alphabetical order.
Example ABCDEFG if your cd rom for example is drive D and you add an USB then this will be drive E
However if you have a network drive that is drive E then your USB will be named drive F etc.
The stiffy drive is drive A, there is no B drive, the hard disk is drive C, the next storage device will be drive D, and the following storage device will be drive E

Bits Bytes and kilobytes *Capacity of data / programs are stored in "Bytes"*
All devices have capacities just like a bin you store your favourite sweeties in.
In computer terminology we refer to capacity as "Bytes, Kilobytes, Megabytes, Gigabytes and Terabytes"

1000 Bytes	= 1KB kilobyte
1000 KB	= 1 MB Megabyte
1000 MB	= 1 GB Gigabyte
1000GB	= 1 TB Terabyte

Below is a screen print of a C drive properties, to view how much space is available

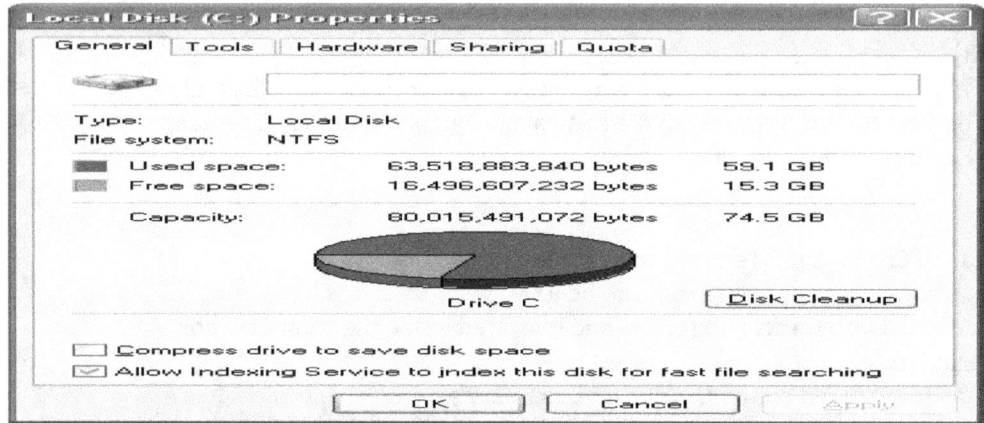

Software

Programs (Software)
Programs are special instructions that are designed to tell the computer what to do.
Some programs are (hardwired) like the BIOS chip whereby instructions are coded electronically onto the BIOS chip. And others are special programs that have been designed to work on the computer. In computer terminology we talk of System software and Application software.
An Application program is a program that has been designed for a specific purpose: for example if you want to write a letter, you need to load the "Letter program" into the computer's memory to work on.

Many programs has been pre-designed and are defined to be off the shelf products that you can go purchase in a computer store and load onto your computer. If you want a special Program that does not exist, you must find a programmer and ask them to design it for you.

The following Application software exists:
Word processing, to type letters with, Example, MS Word, MultiMate, Word perfect
Spreadsheet programs, to do budget sheets with and calculate large amount of numbers with, Example Excel, Quattro-pro, Lotus
Databases, to manipulate large amounts of data with, Example MS Access
Presentation programs, to do presentations with, train people and have meetings with, PowerPoint
Projects to manage multiple projects with, Example MS Projects
Accounting programs, to do financial statements with, Example QuickBooks and Pastel
Specially designed programs, that are designed for a specific business.

Operating systems to manipulate application programs, data and files and control
Instruction on the printer and storage devices are called system programs.

The Operating system (System program)

The operating system is a special program that have been designed to communicate with the hardware devices of the computer. Without the Operating system your computer will not function. The PC need to have an operating system loaded Into the temporary memory storage area in order for the computer to "work " There is different type of operating systems available, just like there are many different Cars in the shops. The following operating systems exist: MS DOS,DR DOS,Unix,OS2,Windows 95,98,ME,2000,XP,Vista and windows 7

The operating system allows the hardware and software programs to communicate with each other and provides control to certain software modules to be loaded onto the computers RAM.

Starting your computer (The boot up sequence)

To start your computer you must press the start button which is usually a small round circle 1 cm in size that is located on your computer. If you press the button again it will switch the computer off. It is not recommended to switch of the computer in this way. *Refer to module 2 on shutting down the computer correctly.*

When you press the Start button on the computer the BIOS will start looking for the operating system. By default (Standard) the bios first look for the operating system on the cd drive and then on the c drive. You can change the boot up sequence that it goes directly to the c drive to locate the operating system IT is advisable to rather keep the original settings.

You should rather not make any changes to the bios setup menu without guidance from a specialist When the bios cannot find the operating system it will display an error message that states <non system disk or disk error> This will happen when the system files are corrupt, damaged or erased. It is possible to accidently delete a system file, or if you left a non bootable stiffy in the stiffy drive.

System files can go corrupt get damaged when you switch off the computer in the incorrect manner You must always close all your programs and use the correct procedure to shut down the pc Never work when there is thunder!!!Unless your boss said, you must work :) There are special devices you can purchase to protect your PC against thunder.

Working with your computer (RAM)

You always work in RAM.RAM is volatile. This means that when the computer shuts down all your hard work is gone. This is why it is important to save your data to permanent storage area like the c drive. Since RAM is only a temporary storage area.

When a user switch on the pc, the bios finds the OS that is loaded on the c drive and loads the needed Files into ram. Not all files are loaded into ram. Only the files you need to work with at the time. When you want to work with other programs the computer close the files that's not needed so that more RAM space is available to work with.
 IT is always a good idea to close programs that you are not working with
 Since if you have less programs open in ram you will be able to access your programs faster. When you purchase a computer, a standard version of windows is provided for you pre-installed. This means you will be able to operate your computer. Remember however that for every program you Wish to work with you need to buy the programs you wish to work with and load it onto the hard disk. You can purchase the Standard MS Office package that include Word excel PowerPoint.

Remember that these programs are not pre-installed on your PC you have to purchase them separately, although some vendors do provide these options for you, some vendors include the software as part of the purchase deal when you buy a PC, and thus load the software for you.

THE COMPUTER

Hardware   Software

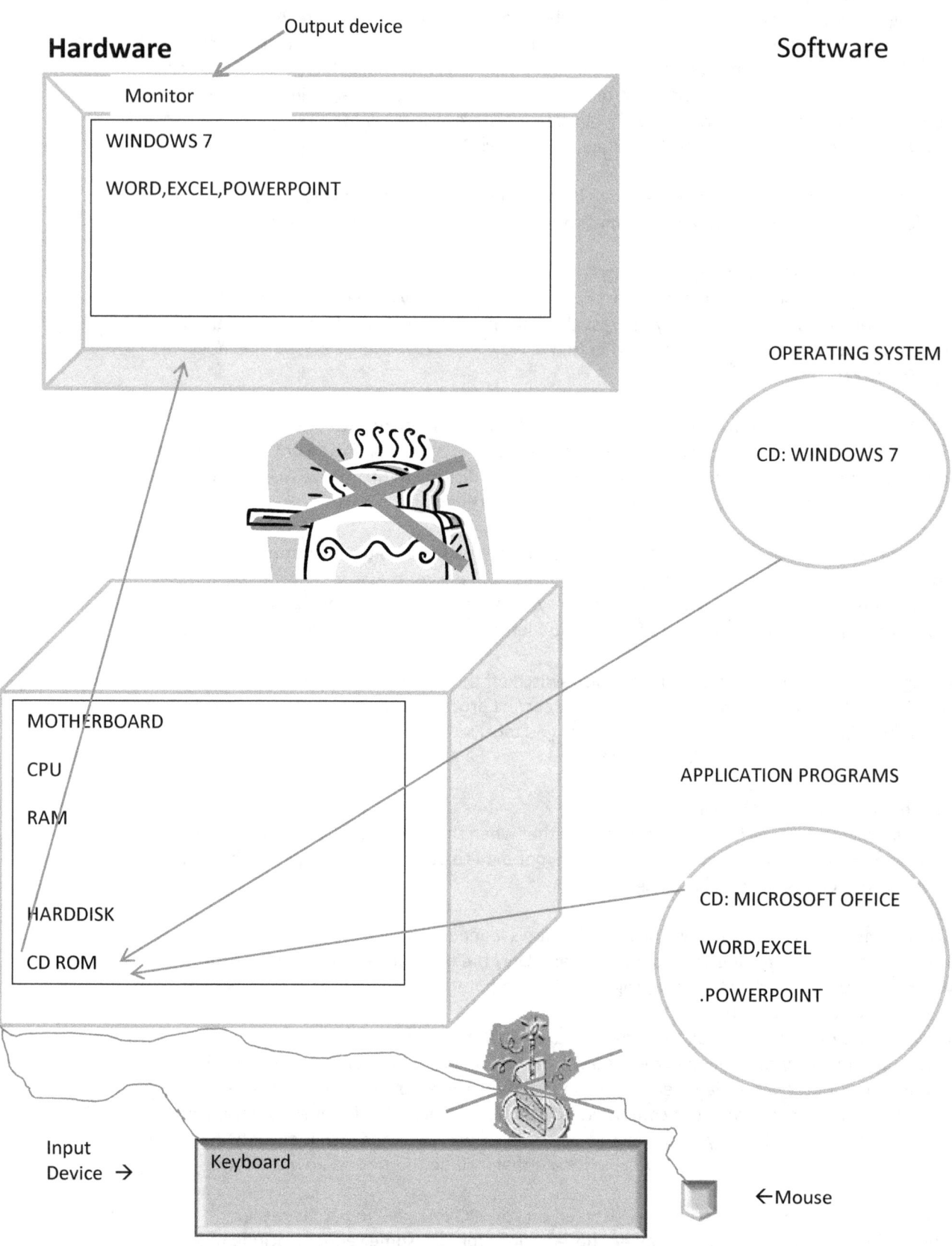

Output device

Monitor

WINDOWS 7

WORD,EXCEL,POWERPOINT

OPERATING SYSTEM

CD: WINDOWS 7

MOTHERBOARD

CPU

RAM

HARDDISK

CD ROM

APPLICATION PROGRAMS

CD: MICROSOFT OFFICE

WORD,EXCEL

.POWERPOINT

Input
Device →   Keyboard   ←Mouse

The input device includes the mouse and keyboard since these provides instructions to the computer.

Keyboard Functions:

Function keys

At the top of the keyboard are function keys F1 – F12 Each function key has a different function in different programs. For example

The F4 function key makes values in excel absolute

The F5 function key moves the cursor to a required position in word and excel

The F1 function key provides help in many programs

Numbers

On the second line of the keyboard are the numbers 1 234567890

There are characters at the top of these numbers !@#$%^&*()_+

To access above numbers press and hold down the SHIFT key and then press the number

For example typing a DOLLAR SIGN $ press and hold the SHIFT key and press the number 4

There are also numbers on the right side of the keyboard, to access these numbers ,

Press the <NUM LOCK> KEY once to activate or deactivate the numbers.

Notice there are arrow keys on these numbers. When the NUM lock key is on, you will be typing in numbers, when the NUM lock key is switched off, the arrow keys will work.

Navigation(Arrow keys and more)

Click on the NUM lock key to switch of the numbers to move the cursor right left up and down by pressing the arrow key that shows that direction.

Press the HOME key will take you to the first character in a line in word, or to the first cell in a row in Excel. Activating an empty cell and pressing the End key and arrow key will move to the last empty cell in excel. In word it will move to the last character in a line. Thus different keys have different functions in different programs, though some could be the same. In some programs you can even assign you own keys to a specific function.

Pressing the PG UP button will move the screen one page up, and PG DN will move the screen one page down.

On many keyboards there are a second set of arrow keys to navigate on the left of the numeric keypad

The ESC key

The ESC key lets you escape out of an action, thus instead of pressing enter to confirm an entry, press ESC to cancel the entry. The ESC key can also removes certain menus from the screen.

The TAB key

The TAB key will sometimes move the cursor to the next entry in a program, or in word it moves the cursor to the right at the TAB stops. *You can learn about TAB stops in the word level 2 manual.*

DEL key

The DEL key will delete(remove) something. When selecting a program in windows explorer and pressing the DEL key it will delete the program. In MS Word it will delete anything in front of the character.

The Backspace key←

The back space key will delete any characters from right where the active cursor are to the left side.

Combination keys

Pressing CTRL ALT DEL , will activate the Task manager. IF your computer program is not working you can fix it with the task manager.

Other combination keys exist in other programs, for example, pressing CTRL S will save a program in Microsoft.

Pressing the Shift key while typing a letter will create a capital letter for that character.

The Caps Lock key

The Caps lock key, will lock the capital letters, providing only capital letters when you type. When you press the Caps lock key it will either switch the capital letters on or off. If you switched the Caps lock on, all the characters you press will be in capital letters, if you then want to type a small letter, once, hold down the shift key while pressing the character, will then produce a small letter. To reverse back to typing only small letters, switch off the caps lock key, by pressing it once.

The Space bar

The space bar is the long rectangular bar on the last line on your keyboard, when you press it in word, it will produce a character space between letters.

The alphabetic characters

The letters are not in alphabetical order, however it is sequenced in a special way, in order for you to be able to type a letter very fast, *some typists can type over 100 letters a minute*. There are special computer programs, that can teach you how to type fast. Or you can go on a typing course to learn how to type the letters faster.

Start menu key

Newer keyboards, have the Start menu build onto a key to quickly activate the start menu in windows.

Short cut menu key

Newer keyboards also have the short cut menu on the keyboard.

Desktop fundamentals   Module 2

Estimated time: 60 minutes

After completion of this module, you will be able to:

- Understand what is a desktop
- Know what is Shortcut icons

- Move shortcut icons
- Delete shortcuts
- Know what is the start menu
- Pin programs to the start menu
- Create a short cut to the desktop
- Know what is the taskbar
- Pin programs to the taskbar

Windows 7

The desktop

After buying your new computer and switching it on,your screen will look similar to the picture below.

This is called <the desktop> and later when you learn to save documents you will learn to save documents to the desktop so it will appear on this screen.

Files and programs that apear on this screen are usualy called <short cut icons> that simply means that a shortcut was created for you to access your file or program from the desktop.

Notice at the left top corner there is a recycle bin, this is where all the data is stored that are deleted on your computer,which means that files that have been deleted can also be restored.

To open a program on your desktop you must (double click)

➢ Click twice with the left mouse button to open a program on the desktop.

The screen layout on the desktop of windows 7 looks similar to Windows XP.

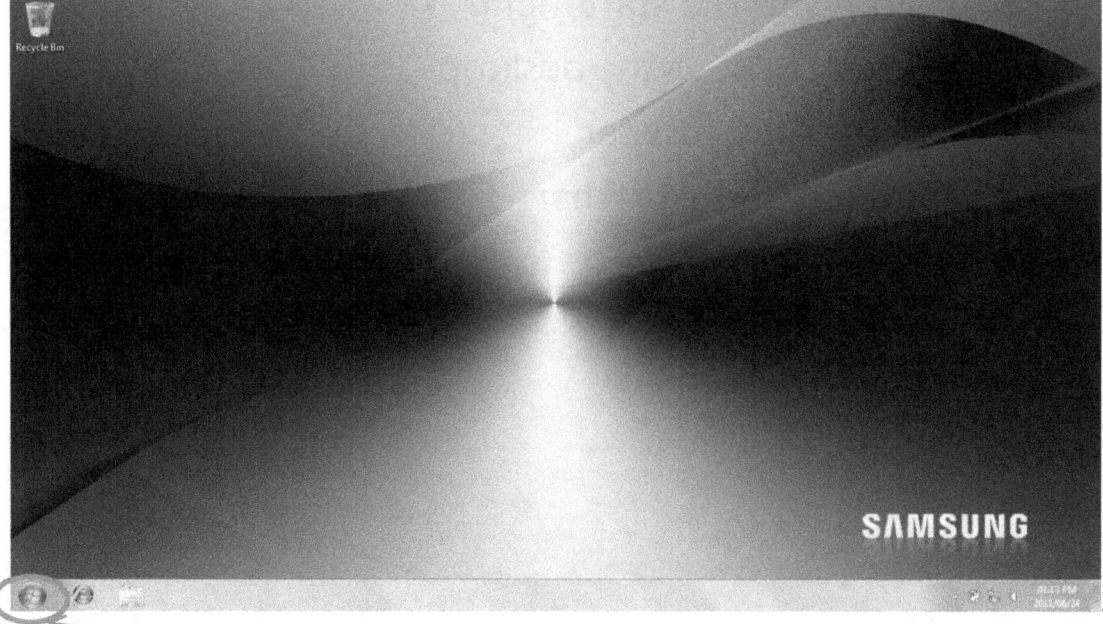

Start menu

At the left corner at the bottom of the screen there is a round circle.

This is called the start button, when you left click on the start button a list of programs will appear.

To open a program on the start menu you simply position the cursor on the program name and then **press the left mouse button once.**

The start menu will show all the recent programs that you have been working on at the top of the start menu. Other programs can be located under the option <all programs>.

You can have a program permanently listed at the top of the start menu by pinning it to the startmenu.

How to pin a program to the start menu

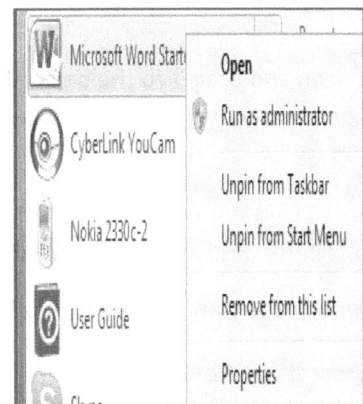

➢ Left click on the start menu
➢ Point to a program you wish to pin (do not left click)
➢ Right click to get the short cut menu
➢ Select <pin to start menu>

Unpin a program from the start menu

➢ Select <unpin from start menu>

Shutting down the computer

There is a special way to switch off the computer by using a function located on the start menu called <shut down>. Switching off the computer at the power button could make your system files go corrupt. When you use the shutdown function, windows close all the programs and store all the system files in the correct places. Using the shutdown function will ensure that your system files won't go corrupt.

➢ Click on start, shutdown
The shutdown function is located on the right side of the start button

To make the start menu go away, simply move the cursor away from the menu and left click on the desktop, or press the ESC key on the keyboard.

Creating a shortcut

Creating a startmenu item on the desktop

If you want to put the program on your desktop, simply point to the desired file and then hold down the left mouse button and move the cursor to the desktop, release the mouse button where you want the shortcut to appear on your desktop. The icon of the program will apear on the screen once the short cut has been created.

Right click on the shortcut on your desktop and choose rename if you want to give it another name.

Moving short cut icons on the desktop

Moving icons manualy

> ➢ Click on the icon and drag it to the desired postion
> *Dragging means to hold down the left button of the mouse while you move the mouse cursor*

Autoarange

Autoarange will align all the icons on the leftside

> ➢ Right click on the desktop and select auto arange

Making icons dissapear from desktop

This action will only make the icons disapear temporarily

> ➢ Right click , select view,click on show desktop icons

> *If there appear a √ next to the show desktop function, it means the <show desktop icon> function is active.*
> *Clicking on it again, will make this function inactive and thus the icons will not appear*

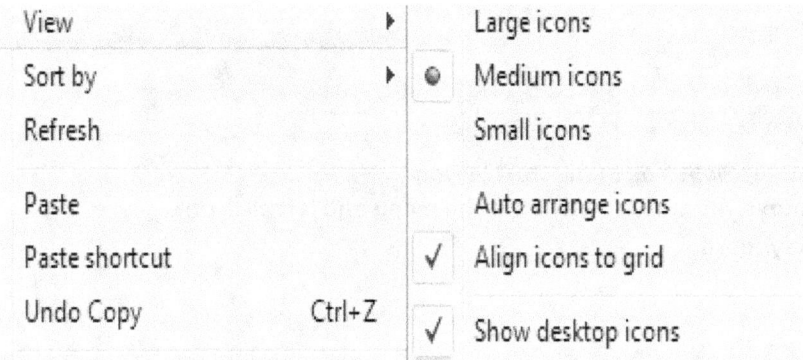

Making icons bigger or smaller

You can change the apearance of the icon by making it bigger or smaller

> ➢ Right click
> ➢ Select <view>
> ➢ Select large,medium or small icons
> *a blue dot will appear next to the item that has been selected, making it the active option*

Deleting short cut icons

This action will remove a short cut icon permanently

> ➢ Left click on the icon, once to select it (remember double click will open the program)
> ➢ Press <delete >on the keyboard

The task bar

Next to the start button, there is a grey bar appearing to the right side at the bottom of the screen this is called the taskbar. When you open programs, the program icon will appear on the taskbar indicating that this program is now open in RAM and you are busy with this program.

Pinning a program to the taskbar means that this program will be accessible to you on the taskbar when you start your computer.

How to pin a program to the taskbar

➢ When you right click on any of the start menu options, there will be an option available:
➢ Pin to taskbar (left click on this option to pin it to the taskbar)

More items on the taskbar (the sound function)

On the right corner of the taskbar there are some additional functions

One of them is called the <sound function>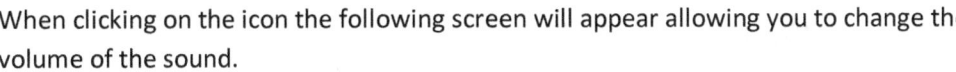

When clicking on the icon the following screen will appear allowing you to change the volume of the sound.

➢ Dragging the bar up will increase the volume
➢ Dragging the bar down will decrease the volume
➢ To make the menu go away, click anywhere on the desktop away from it

Left click on the date and time to change it

Notebook batteries

If you have a notebook, the amount of battery capacity will also be listed on the right hand side of the taskbar, click on the icon to reveal the amount of battery capacity left.

More options

If there are more options on your taskbar, an up arrow will appear, when you click on it, it will reveal more programs

Changing the time and date

At the right side at the bottom the date and time appear, you can change the date and time

Changing the date

➢ Left click, where the date are displayed
➢ Click on change date and time
➢ Click on the correct date to change the date
➢ Click on the right or left arrow to change the month

Changing the time

↓ Click inside the rectangular square where the time is indicated and type in the new time or
↓ Click on the up or down arrow to increase or decrease the time

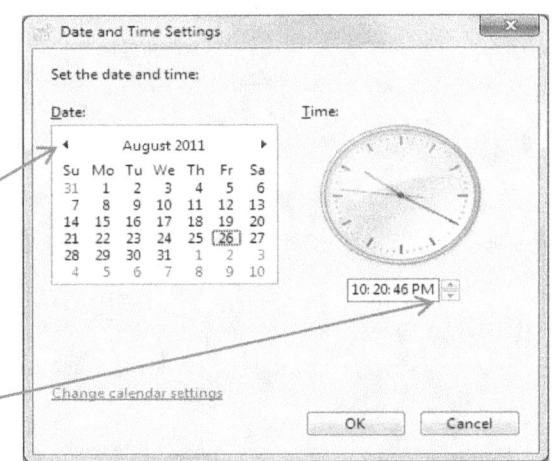

Exploring Windows

Module 3

Estimated time: 30 minutes

After completion of this module, you will be able to:

- Understand what is a window
- Move a window
- Resize a window
- Minimize maximize and close a window
- Cascade windows
- Stack windows

Exploring <u>windows</u>

Click on the start menu to activate the windows explorer
Or at the search option type in <explore> or
Right click on the start menu and select <open windows explorer>

Windows explorer is a program that allows you to view everything on your computer. With windows 7 you have libraries included in the explorer.

You can browse all the existing folders and files and create new folders and libraries with windows explorer, it is advisable to pin this program to the task bar or start menu since you might use it again.

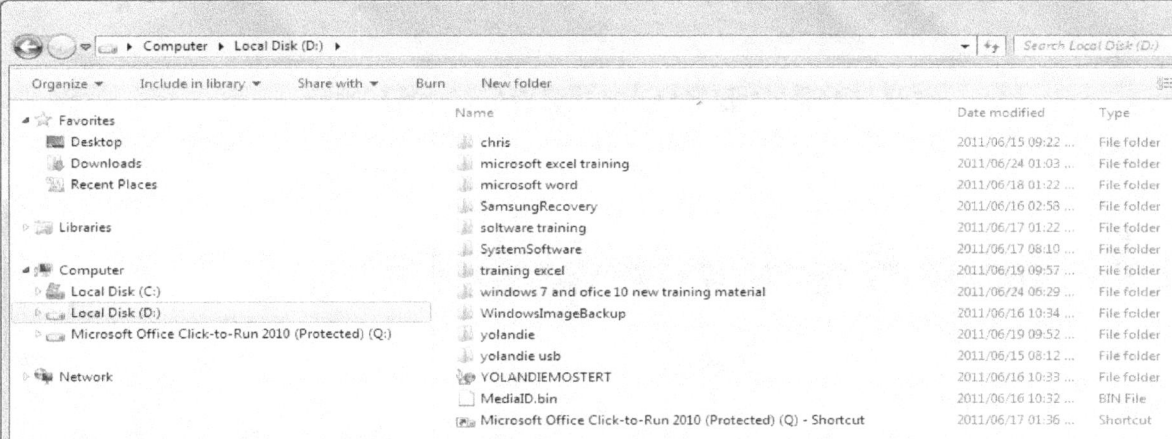

Resizing a Window dialog box

The above square is called a window dialog box. Most programs and functions work within a window. Most functions of a window dialog box are the same. When you move the cursor to the border line it will change to an arrow key indicating that you can resize the (square) window dialog box. While holding down the left mouse button move the cursor to the right to increase the window size or move it to the left to decrease the window size.

Dragging the cursor left right up or down will decrease or increase the size of the dialog box.

Moving a window dialog box

The top blue line is called the title bar and when you position the cursor in the centre of the blue line at the top, you will be able to move the dialog box. Hold down the left button and move the mouse cursor to the position where you want to move the dialog box to and then release the mouse button.

Cascading and stacking windows

When you have more than one program open in memory, you can cascade, stack or show the windows side by side on one screen.

Cascading Windows

Cascading is when the title bar of all the programs is visible, so that you can quickly click on it to make it the active window to work on.

- ➢ Right click on the taskbar *on a clean area, not on a program icon*
- ➢ Select cascade windows

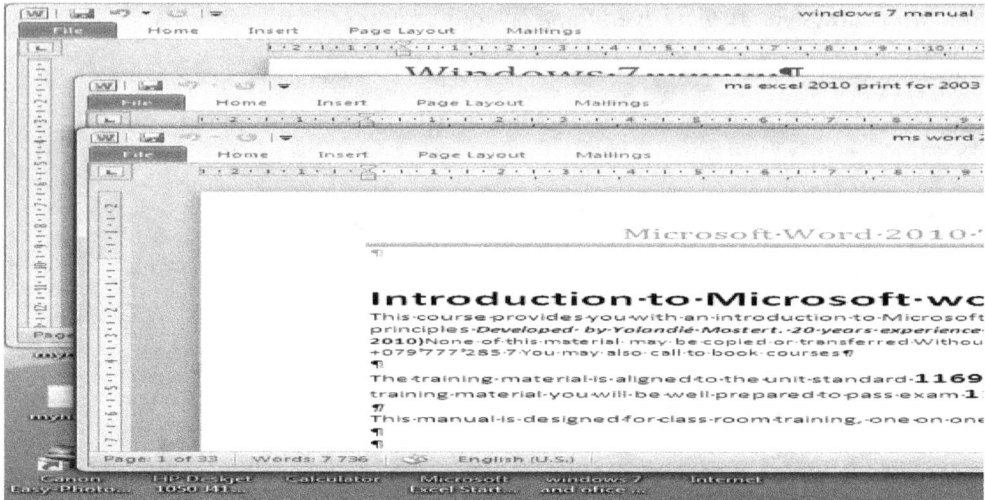

Stacking windows

Stacking windows is when, all the programs that are in memory are visible onscreen underneath each other

- ➢ Right click on the taskbar
- ➢ Select show windows stacked

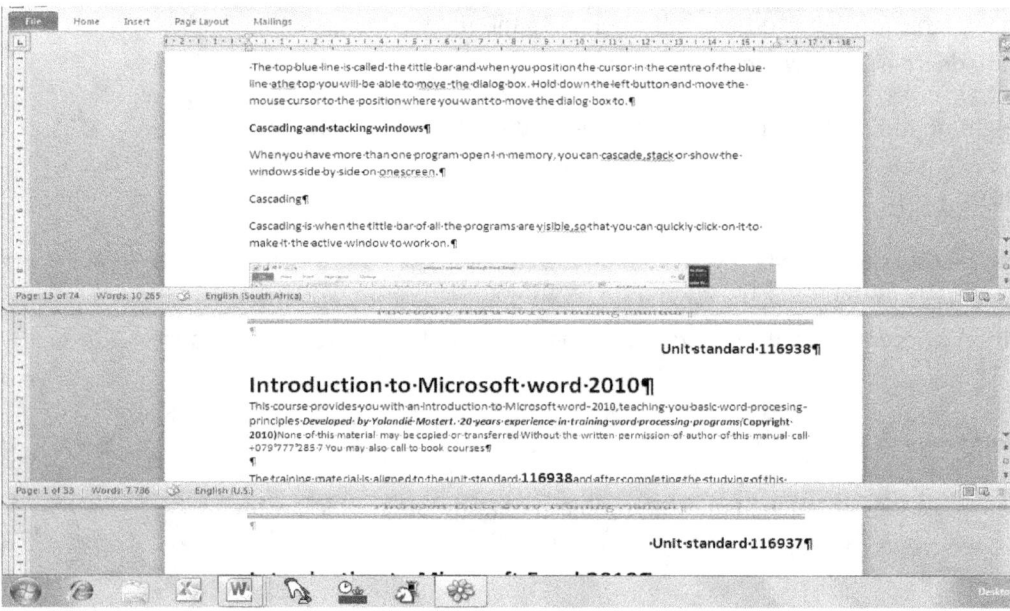

Show window side by side

You can also view the programs that are in memory, side by side on the screen

> ➢ Right click on the taskbar
> ➢ Select show windows side by side

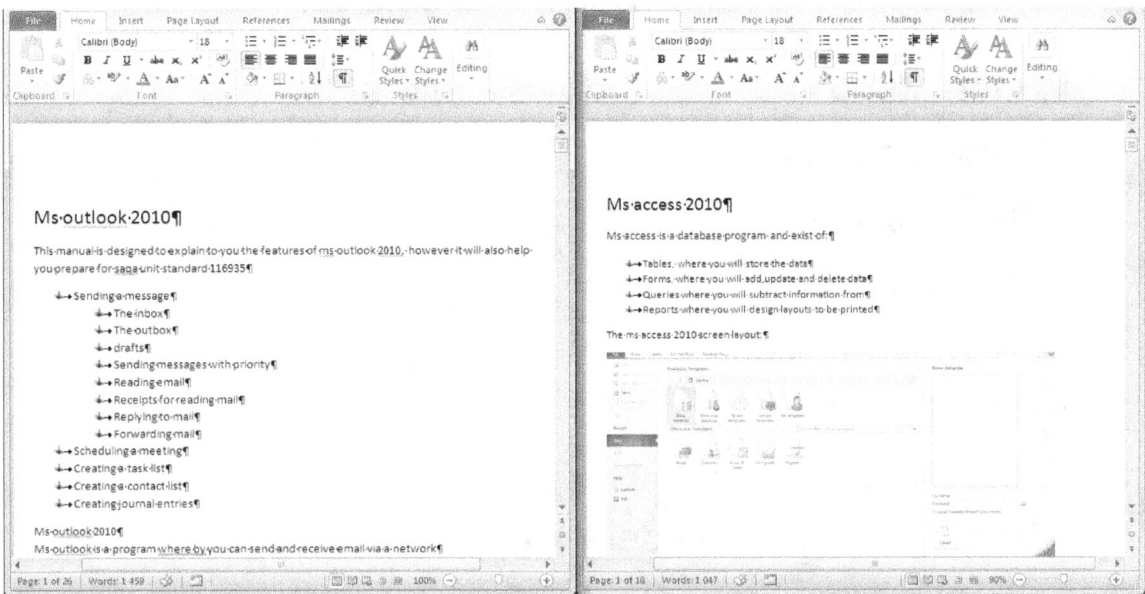

The minimize maximize and close button

Most of the time ,On the right side of the screen you will find the min max and close button,
This will close the program or minimize or maximize the program.

The minimize button

The minimize button will minimize the program,so that it is no longer visible on the screen, you can open the program on the screen by clicking on it at the bottom of the screen, this is called the taskbar. All programs that are still open in memory are located on the taskbar.

The maximize button

When your screen has been reduced to half the size or less than full size,you can click on the maximize button to expand the program so that it can apear full screen.

The close button Closing the program

Clicking on the close button will make the program disapear from your screen and it **will no longer be in the memory** and thus not be available on the taskbar(*unless you pinned it to the taskbar*).To restart your program you will have to go to the start buton or the desktop or *click on the taskbar. You can also press ALT F4 to close the program.*

Managing Files and Folders   Module 4

Estimated time: 80 minutes

After completion of this module, you will be able to:

- Understand what is windows explorer
- Browsing folders
- Browsing files
- Creating folders
- Creating subfolders
- Filtering files
- Searching for data
- Moving copying and deleting files
- Creating libraries

Windows Explorer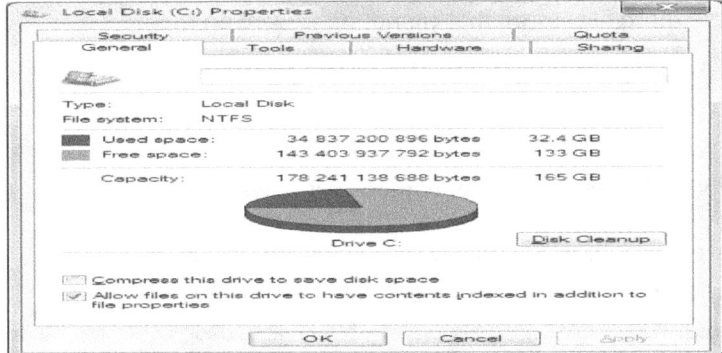

On the left side of the **windows explorer** you will find the C drive(local disk)

The C drive(hard disk)

The hard disk is the permanent storage area of the computer. Each computers file capacity may differ.

When you are in the windows explorer you can right click on the c drive and select< properties> to identify the capacity of the disk.

Some computers have more than one hard disk and others only have 1. If you only have one disk you can also partition your hard disk to split it into 2 pieces. Thus creating a virtual C and D drive.

When you double click on the C local drive, the view will be expanded and you will be able to view all the folders that have been saved on the C drive.

When you double click on the C drive again the view will collapse and folders won't be visible.

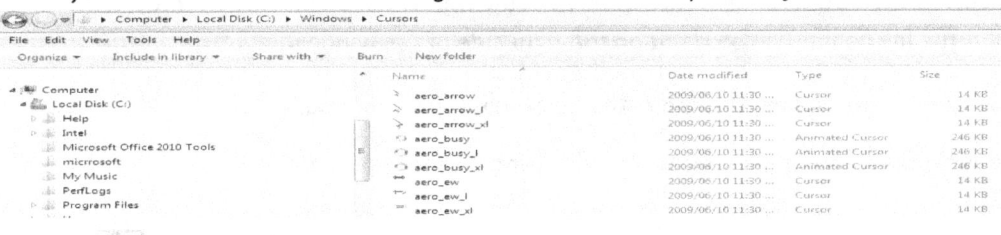

Folders

Folders are cabinets in which files are stored in, you can create your own folders to store information. Many of the system files that are stored on your computer has been organized into different folders. If you wish to see the content of a folder, click on it and you will see the content of that folder on the right side. Usually on the right side you will find the sub folders and the files.

Files

A file is a document that has been created in a specific program, each file have a 3 letter extension specifying in which program it has been created. For example Ms word has a doc and excel is xls and notepad is txt extension. Mp3 and wav is sound files. Ppt is PowerPoint files.jpg,bmp ,tif and gif are picture files. When you save files you may not use the following characters <>?:"{} inside the filename. You can easily identify a file by its icon, all programs have different icons to identify it, MS word has a big blue

W and Microsoft excel has a big green **X** indicating it is an excel document. It is best to organize your files into folders. Files are usually located within folders on the right side of the window dialog box

Browsing files and folders

The windows explorer, will list the drives and folders on the left side of the screen and the contents of the folders on the right side of the screen. The window is divided by a vertical line.

If there is more information on the left side of the screen that cannot be displayed on the screen, an up and down arrow will appear with a vertical dark grey bar. This is the scroll bar and when you drag it up or down you will be able to view data at the top or bottom of the screen. A scroll bar will also appear on the right side of the screen when there are more files listed that cannot be viewed on the screen.

Browsing windows system files

Windows has its system files stored on the c drive located under the folder named <windows>.

It is important that you never try to move these system files or delete them. These files are loaded onto your hard disk and when you boot up your computer it loads the necessary system files into memory so that you can operate your computer. Deleting or moving these system files will cause your operating system not to function properly. It is important to never delete any files that you have not created yourself, because you can accidently delete an important program file.

When you double click on the C drive you will find all the folders listed on the left side of the window, when you click on one of these folders, the subfolders will be located on the right side. The right side of the window shows the contents of what has been selected on the left side. Thus if there are files inside the subfolder the file names will be listed on the right side of the window.

Some of the folders will contain an arrow key; this indicates that it contains subfolders

Double clicking on this folder will make the sub folders appear or disappear on the left side of the screen

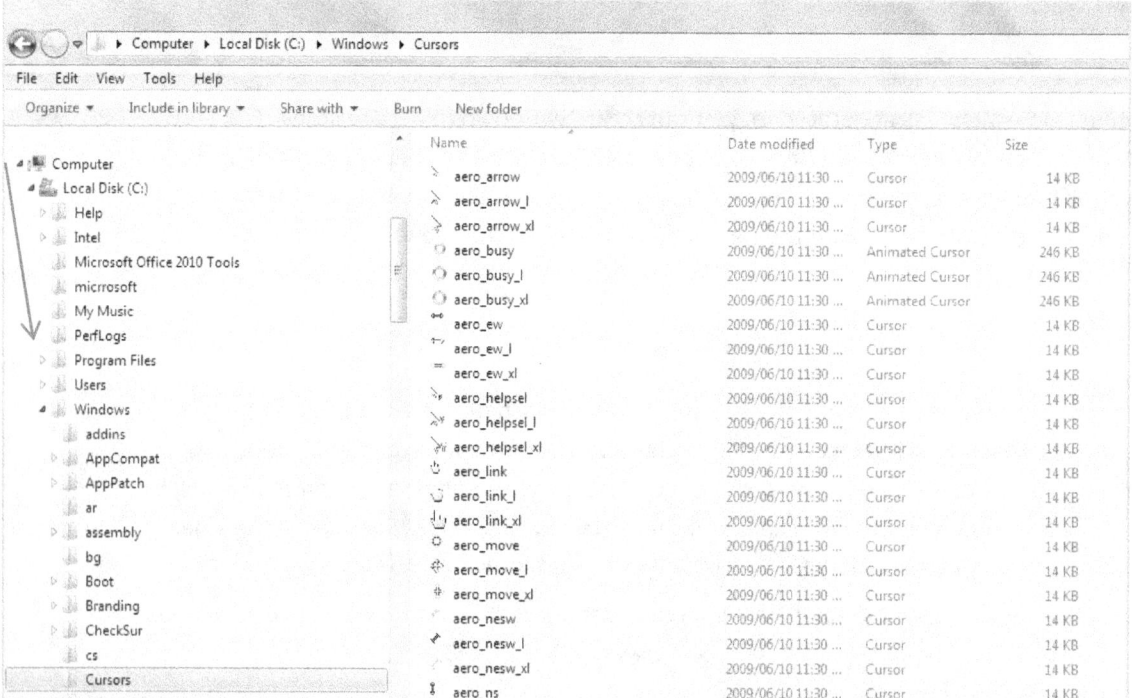

Browsing program files

You will notice on your c drive there is a folder called program files. Many of the program names that are listed on the start menu are available within the program files folder. The program files folder is where all the program files are located. Windows use these files to open programs into memory when you wish to work with it. Please do not move any of these files. If you delete these files your program might not work effectively anymore.

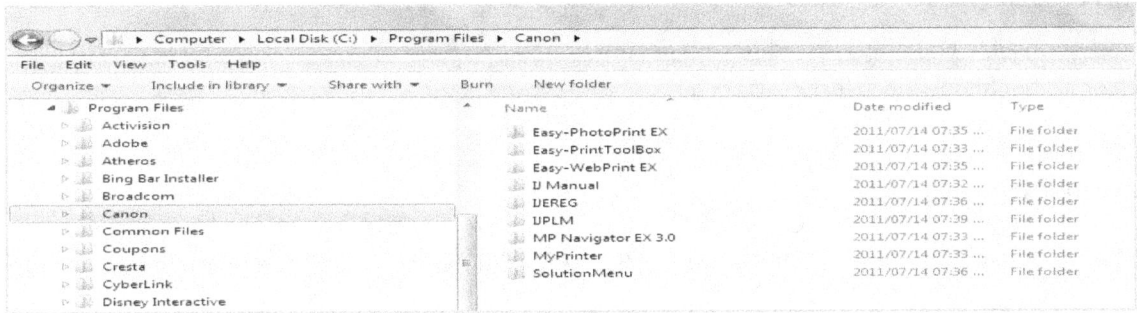

Viewing other files and folders

Clicking on <computer> on the left side of the window will list all the drives for you on the right side.

Double click on the drive of your choice to view the contents of the drive.

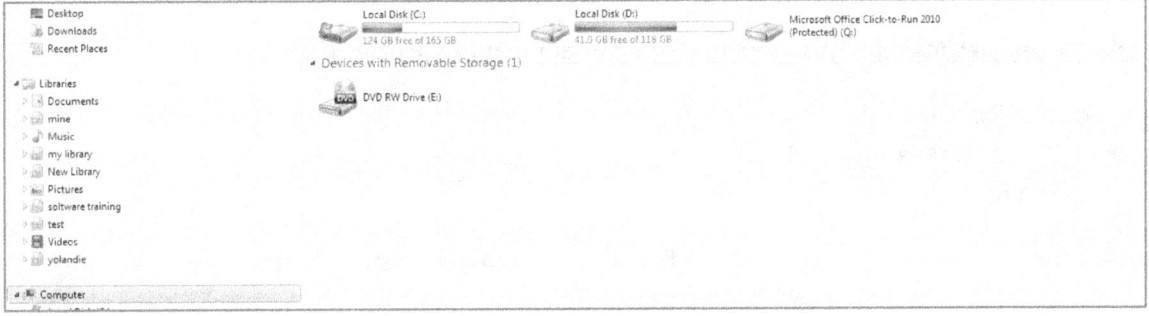

How to create your own folder

➤ Click on the D or C drive and select <file> <new folder>
➤ Type in the name of your new folder and press <enter>
   The name <new folder> will be replaced with the name that you have typed in.

Creating sub folders

To create a sub folder simply select the folder where you wish to place the sub folder in, and click on <file> ,<new folder>
Writing C:\manuals\word\level 1 means that <manuals> is a main folder and <word> is a subfolder of <manuals> and <level 1> is a sub folder of <word>.
To create a subfolder inside the <word> folder called <level 2> you have to select the <word> folder first, before you select, file new folder.

Compressed files and folders

You can compress files by sending files to a special compressed folder, the result will be that the file will be much smaller to transport.

- ➢ Select the file or folder
- ➢ Right click and select send to
- ➢ Select compressed folder

Uncompressing files:

- ➢ Double click on a file and drag it to a different destination
- ➢ Right click on the folder and select <extract all>

Moving files and folders

When you hold down the left button of the mouse, you can drag a file or folder to a new destination

You can also move more than one item at a time.

You can also move files by using the cut command

- ➢ Select a file, right click, select <cut>
- ➢ Position the cursor on the folder where you want to move the file to.
- ➢ Left click on the folder to select it
- ➢ Right click, select paste

Selecting adjacent files(selecting more than one file that is underneath each other)

- ➢ Click on the first file
- ➢ Press the SHIFT key on the keyboard, hold it in
- ➢ Click on the last file

Selecting non adjacent files(selecting more than one file, that is not underneath each other)

- ➢ Click on the first file
- ➢ Press and hold the CTRL key on the keyboard
- ➢ Click on all the files you want to select

Copying files

You can make a duplicate copy of a file for backup purpose

- ➢ Select a file, right click, select <copy>
- ➢ Position the cursor on the folder where you want to paste the copy of the file
- ➢ Left click on the folder to select it
- ➢ Right click, select paste

Deleting files and folders

When you want to delete files that you no longer want on your system you can remove them

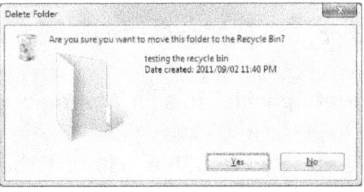

- ➤ Select the files or folders that you want to delete and
- ➤ **Press< delete> on the keyboard**
  Deleting a folder will remove all the subfolders and files within it

These files will be moved to the recycle bin where you can permanently delete them or you can restore them to the original destination.

Recycle bin

On the desktop left top you might find the recycle bin. Double click to open the program.

A list of all the files and folders that has been deleted will be viewable.

At the top of the window you find the following options:

Empty recycle bin will permanently **remove all the files** on your computer.

Restore all items will restore the items to its original location.

If you wish to restore or delete only certain files you need to **select them** and then click on restore
The restore function will change to selected items only

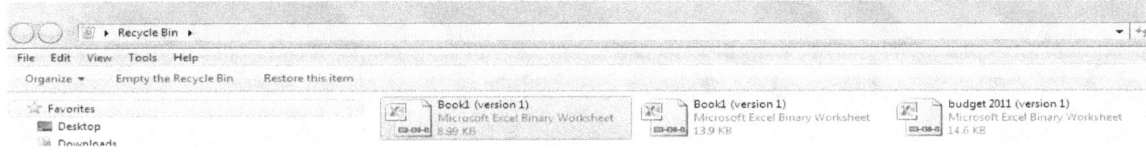

Permanently deleting files

- ➤ Select the files in the recycle bin
- ➤ Press <delete> on the keyboard
- ➤ Click on <yes> to permanently delete the files or folders selected

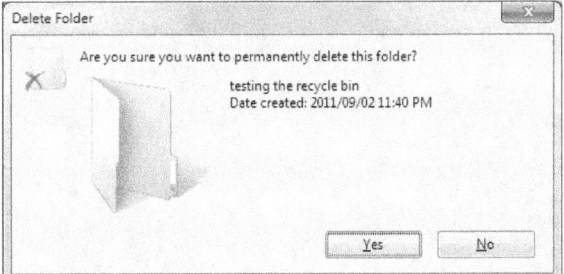

Libraries

A library is a way in which your data is organised so that you can **view** your data easier.

Libraries are not included in the windows XP and NT operating systems.

When deleting a FILE in a library the original document in the original folder will also be deleted.

When deleting a FOLDER in a library the original folder and contents still remain on your drive, you merely are deleting the link, thus the folder are no longer included in the library.

You can either store data to one of the existing libraries listed below or you can create your own library.

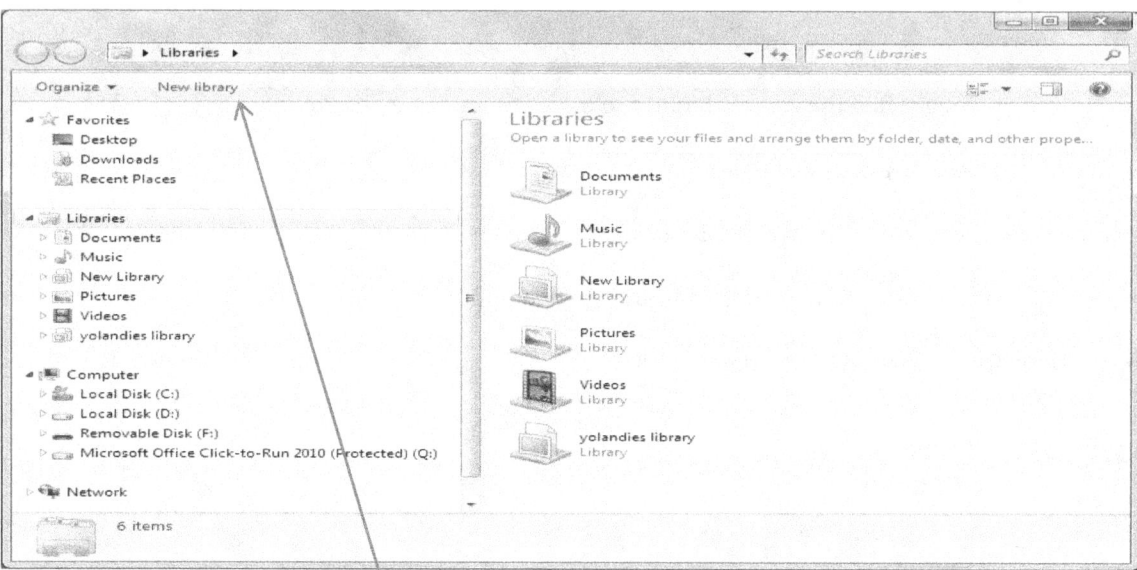

How to create your own library

> Step 1 Click on NEW LIBRARY to create a new library

> Step 2 Click on Include folder and select the folder you want to add to the library

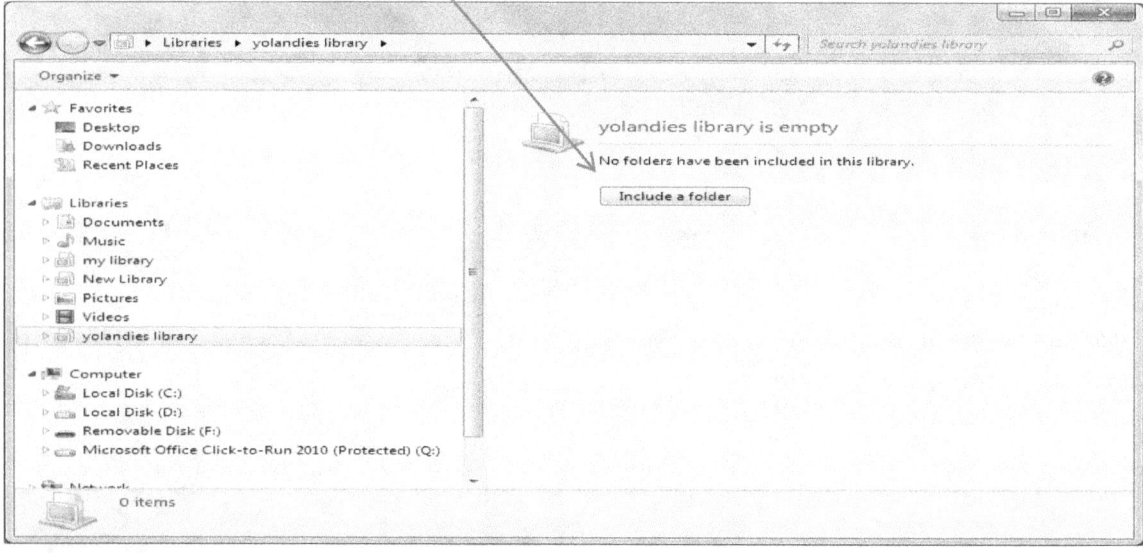

To add more folders to a library

- ➢ Click on the folder you want to add
- ➢ Click on <include in library>
- ➢ Select the library name of your choice, by left clicking on it once

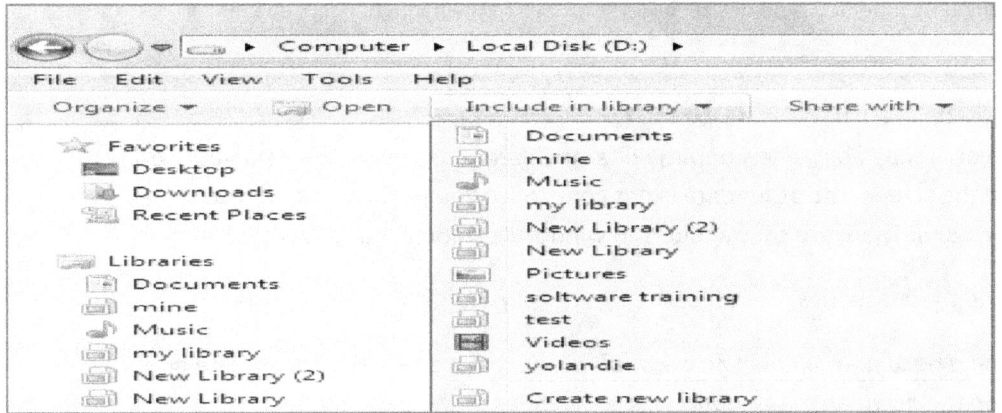

After adding a folder with files into your library the results would look like below

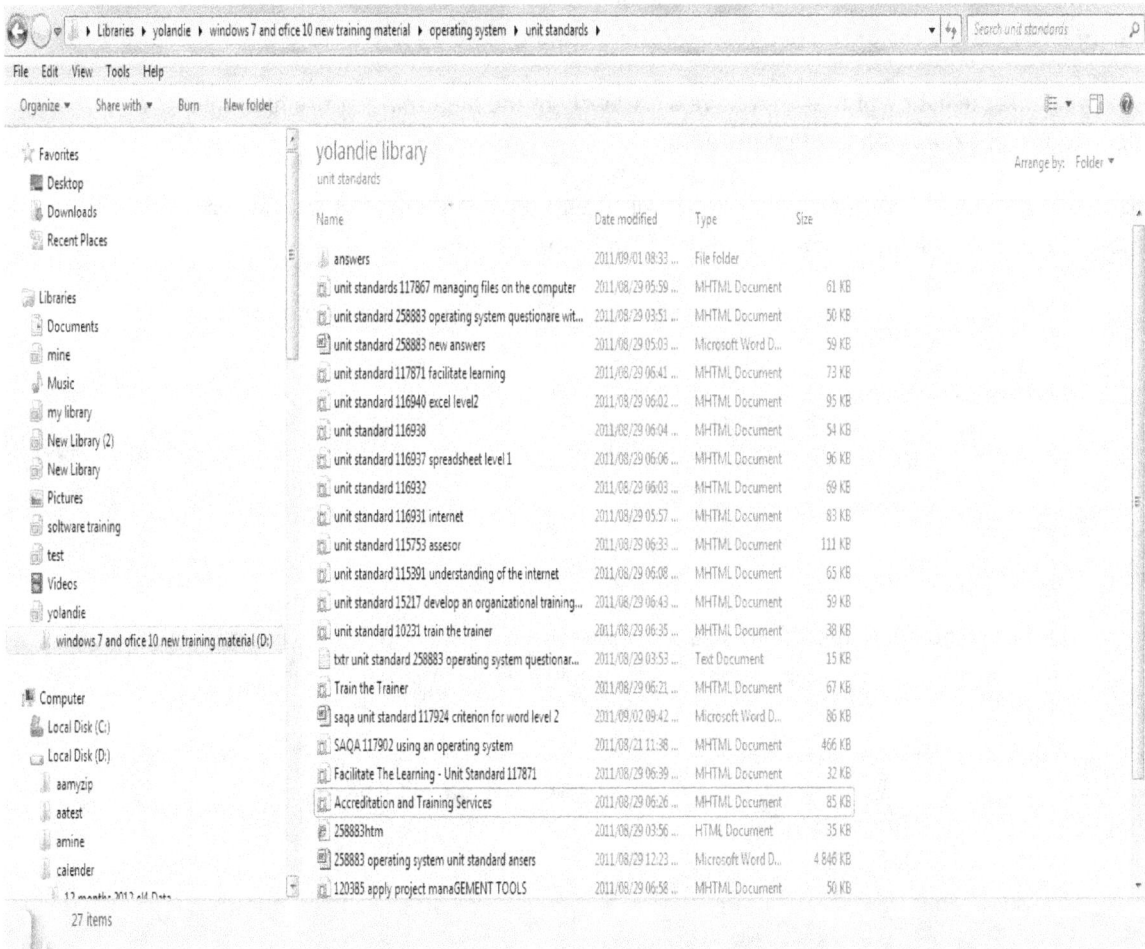

When browsing your folders on the C or D drive an option on the main menu will be available to include your folder to a library, you can at any time include a new or existing folder to a library.

Sorting Files

➤ Right click on the start menu and select windows explorer

You can sort your files by,Name,date modified,type or size, by left clicking on the name headers above

Filtering file names in windows **explorer**

Filtering data, means that you will be able to temporarily filter the data so that only the data you are looking for will be listed on the screen, the other data is not gone, once you remove the filter the rest of the data will appear again. There are special filters in windows explorer that you may use.

On the right side of the pane the file names are listed.

Notice that next to the <name header> is a down arrow, most of the times down arrows indicate an option list. When clicking on the down arrow an option list will appear to choose from.

You can select <a – h> this will list all the files from <a> alphabetically sorted up to <h>,thus file names that start with the letter a will be at the beginning of the search filter and the filter will stop at the last file name that has an <h> at the beginning of the filename.

Selecting <I – p> will start the listing of files that have a letter <I> in the beginning of the filename and the last file listed will be files with the first letter <p>

Selecting <q to z> will start listing files who's filenames begin with the letter <q>. the last file listed will be filenames that contain the letter <z> at the beginning of the filename.

Click inside the little squared box to select your chosen filter. An √ icon will appear inside the box

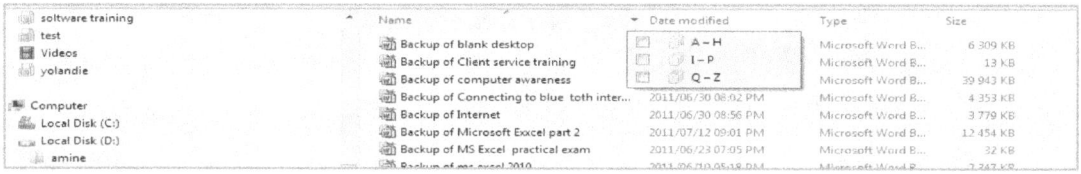

Filtering dates

Click on the down arrow next to <date modified> and click inside the squared box to select your date filter

An √ will indicate that the option is selected, clicking in the checkbox again will deactivate the option

Selecting a range of dates

More than one item is called a range, to select more than one date do the following

➢ Click on the first date you wish to include in your search, hold down the left button of the mouse and move the cursor over all the dates you wish to include in the filter

Only the files that match the date filter will be listed

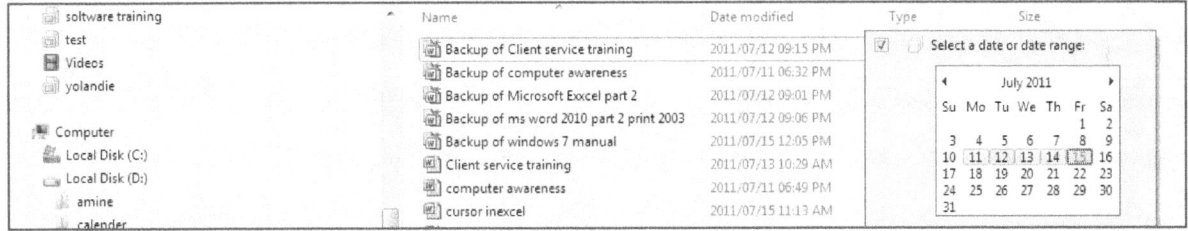

Filtering files by type

Click on the down arrow next to the word <type> and choose from the option list which type of document you want to search for. You can select a word document, backup document, excel document, pdf adobe acrobat or, rich text format document. Click inside the checkbox to select file types

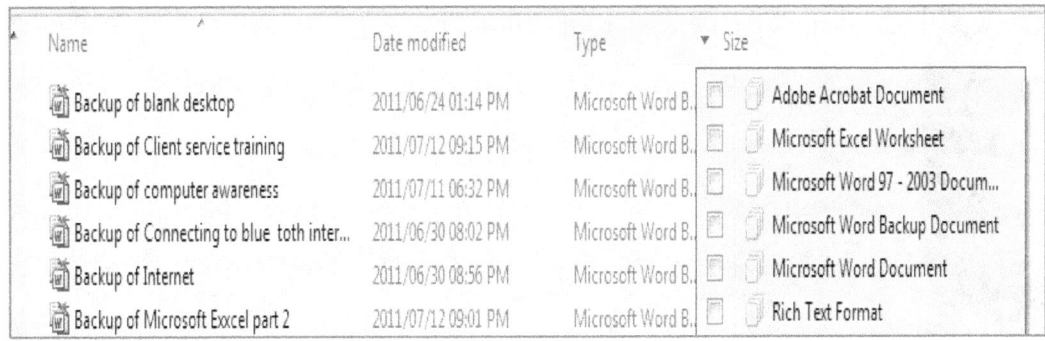

Filtering files by size

You can filter by choosing, small medium large or huge files.

Click inside the checkbox to select the file size

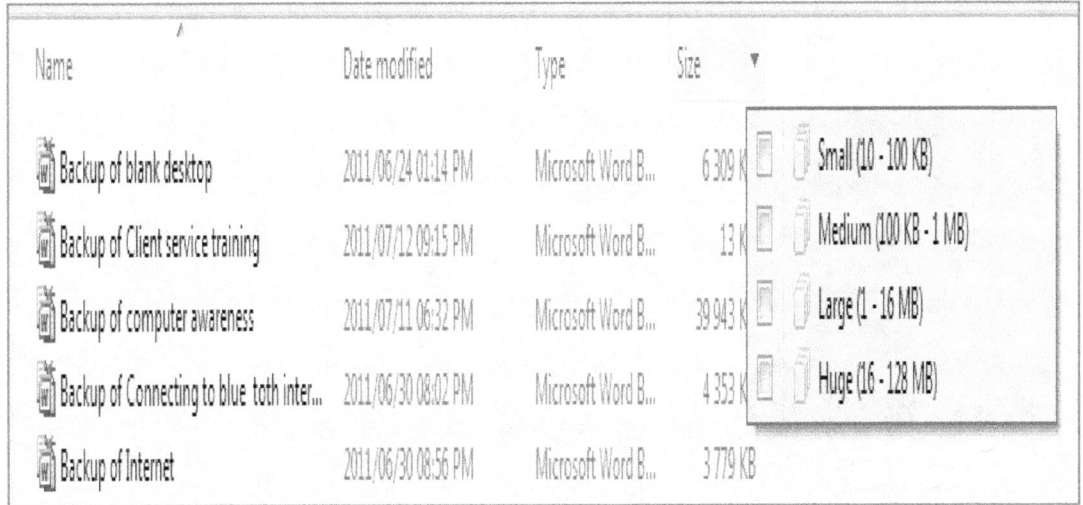

On the right side of the pane there are more options available

View options

The view options will change the way you look at your information

  ➤ Click on the <u>down arrow</u> next to the view options to select more options

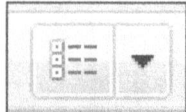

The following options will appear:

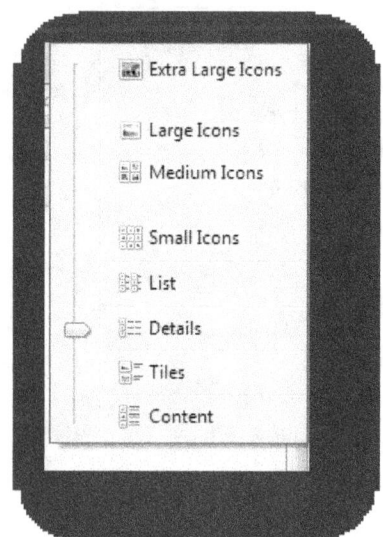

Extra-large icons will make the icons appear larger

Large icons are smaller than extra-large icons

Medium icons are smaller than large icons

Small icons are the smallest icon

List items will list the documents in words

Details will provide the file size and file type and date modified

Content provide the author details and file size and date

Clicking on the <?> question mark will provide the help menu

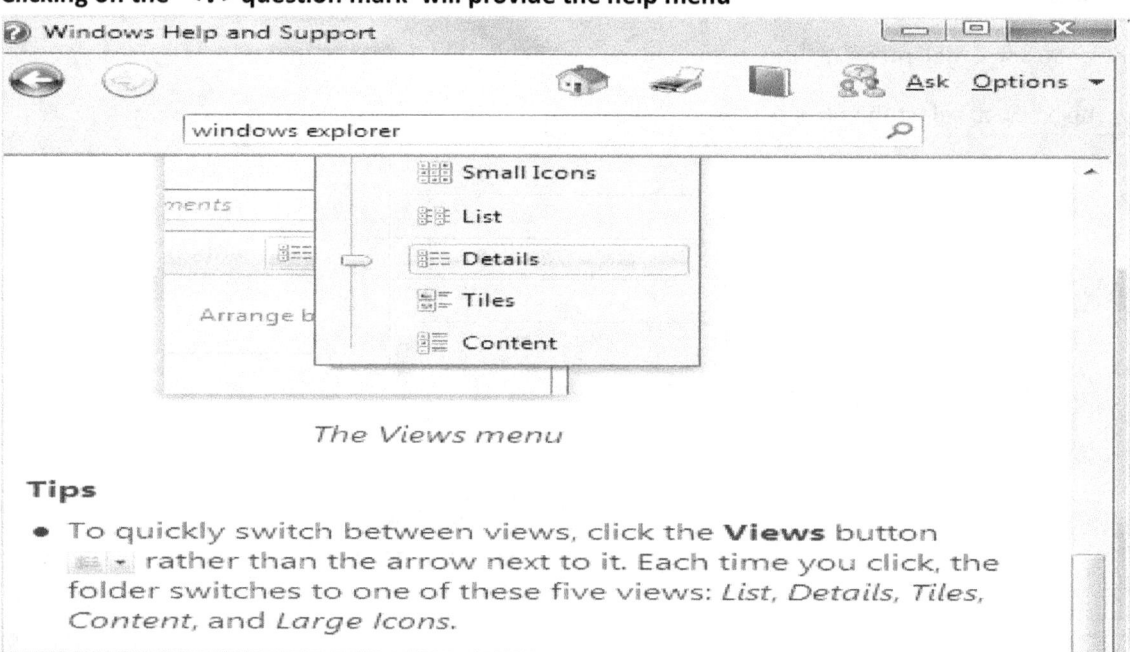

Search with windows explorer

The search option in windows explorer allows you to quickly search for files within certain folders or find information on any device connected to your computer.

At the right side of the screen at the top, the search option appears, simply type in the search criteria, however ensure to select where the search should take place.

When a folder is selected, search will take place within that folder.

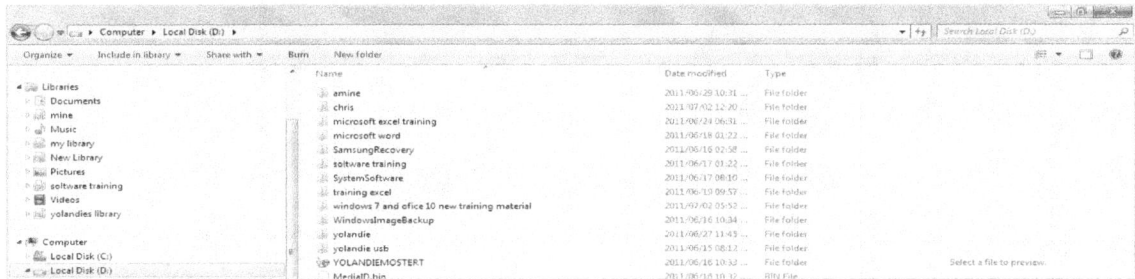

You can search for information by using a search filter, or search by date modified or by size

Search filters

Practise exercise: Search for training documents

  ➢ Click on <computer> to identify that all drives connected to the computer will be searched
  ➢ Left click inside the search area at the right top corner of the screen
  ➢ Type in the word <training> and press enter

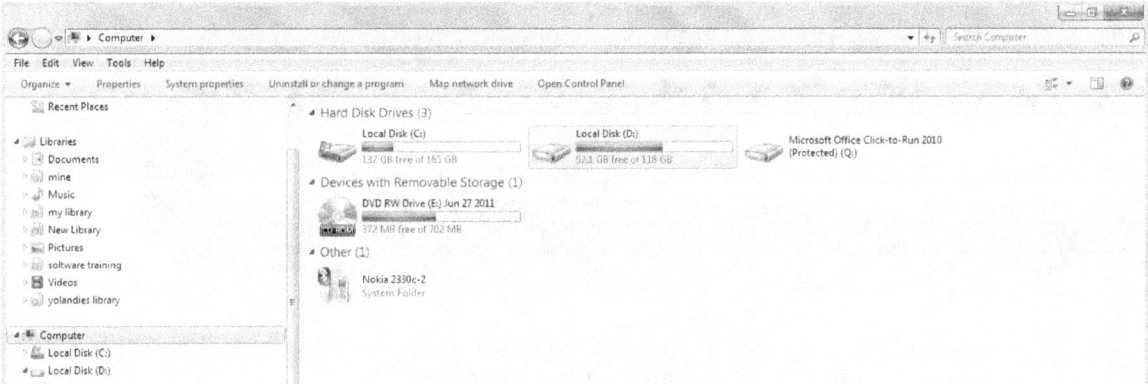

Results of training search: *Notice that the word training is highlighted*

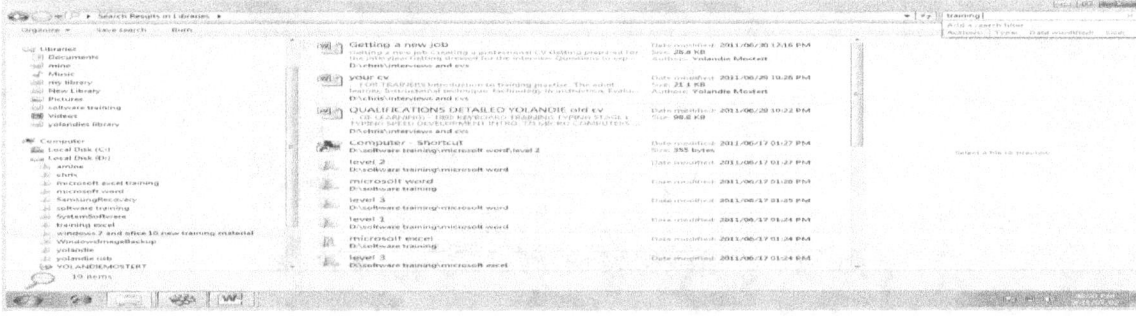

If information searching for was not found in the location you can change the search criteria

By selecting a different drive to search for or alter the search information

> Click on custom to identify the folders that should be included in the search.
> Click inside the checkbox to add an item to the search.

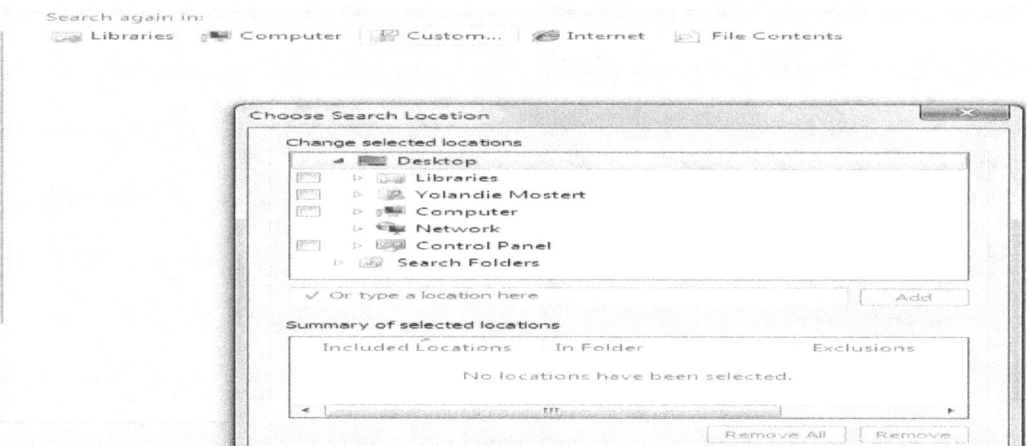

To search for Microsoft word documents that start with the letter <y>

> Open windows explorer
> Left click inside the search area at the right top corner of the screen
> Type in <Y*.doc> *The star indicates any characters, thus documents starting with Y will be listed*
> Press <enter>

Search selection

You can also select the following searches located at the right top search menu

Searching by kind

Select whether it is a file or folder or what kind of information you are looking for

Searching by type

You can select the type of document you are searching for, for example doc is a word document and xls is an excel document. Select <library>, and select <type> at the search criteria and click on the type of document you desire

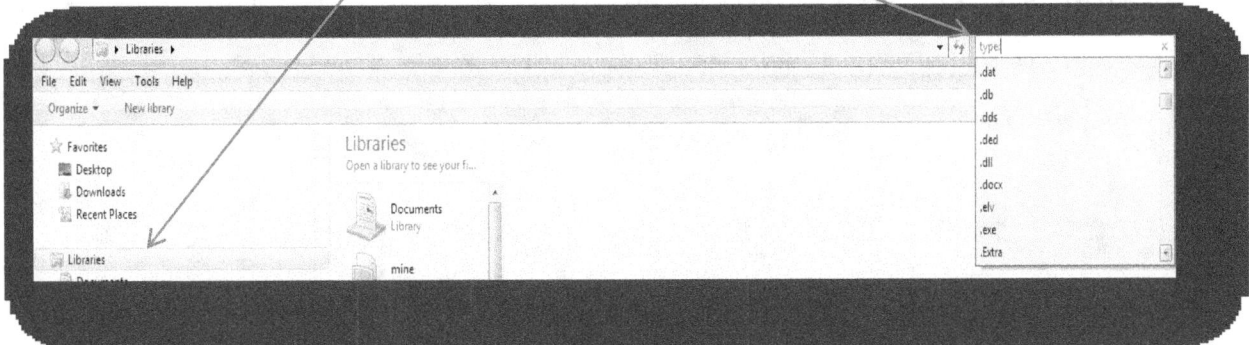

Searching by date modified

You can specify a date range to search for your information

➢ Click on date modified and select the date range, or type in date modified: and left click once.

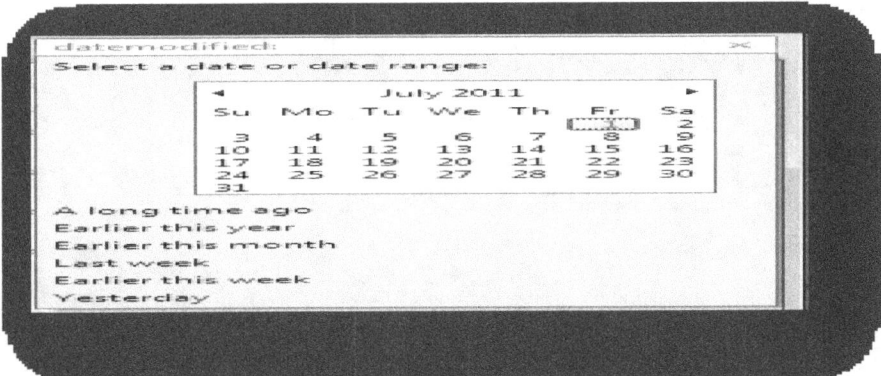

Searching by size

You can search documents according to their size, for example small, large or gigantic

➢ Within the search option type in <size:> and left click once

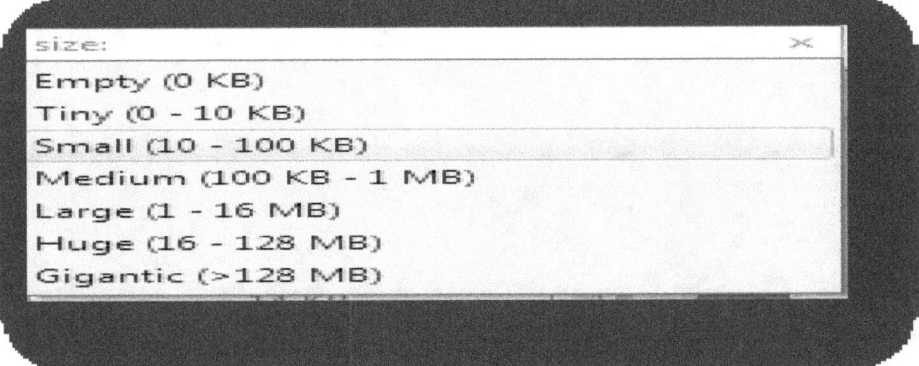

Using Help.

➢ Click on START, HELP and SUPPORT

➢ You can also press F1 to get the help menu

➢ Or click on the question mark within windows explorer

In the HELP dialog box you can either search for specific information or you can browse by content listed.

You can click on any of the information listed below and it will display help information about the topic

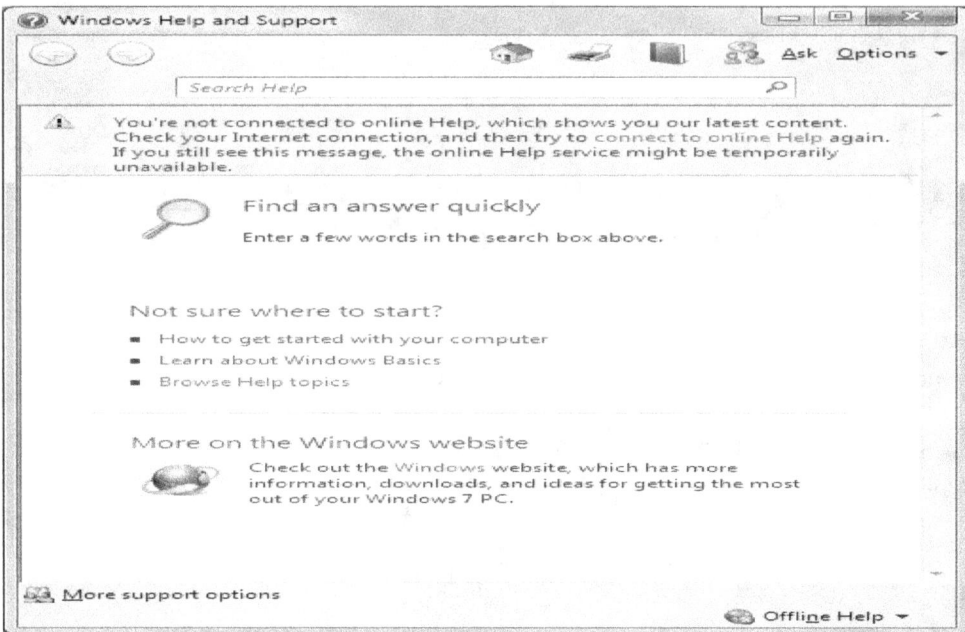

Practise exercise: Windows Help and Support

➢ Click inside the search area and type in <shut down> and press enter.

➢ Select the first option: Shutting down your computer properly.

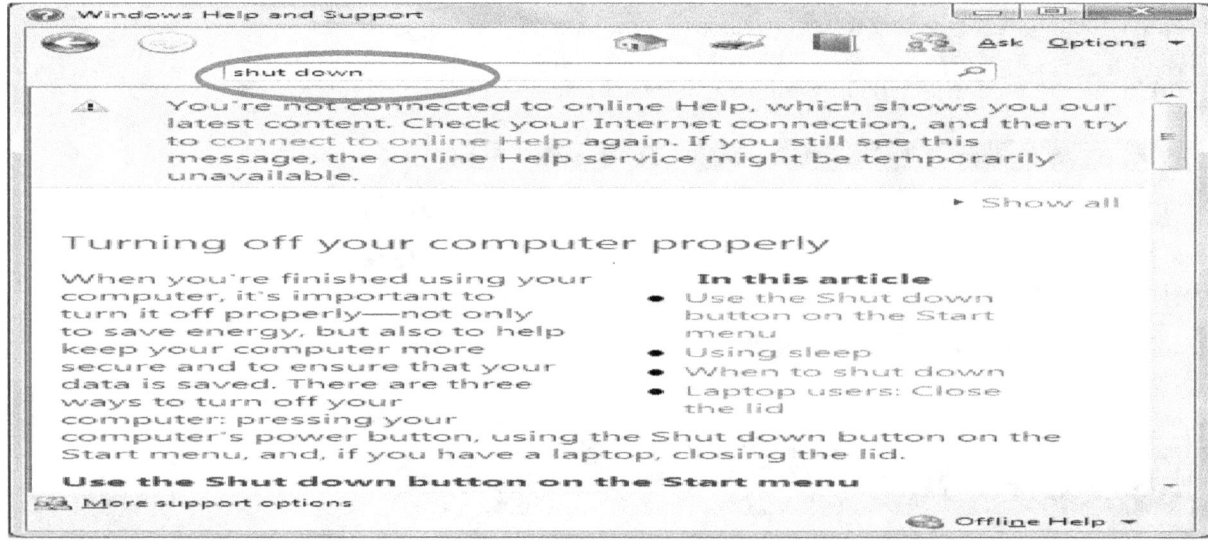

Control Panel   Module 5

Estimated time: **120 minutes**

After completion of this module, you will be able to know what is:

- Window updates
- Power options
- Backup and Restore
- Firewall
- Using internet via Bluetooth
- Adding printers
- Installing and uninstalling programs
- Screen saver
- Changing desktop background
- Changing the mouse settings
- Changing currency, date and time
- Sound settings
- Remote assistance
- Defragment a disk
- User accounts
- Parental control
- Speech recognition

Control panel

With the control panel you can change the settings on your computer

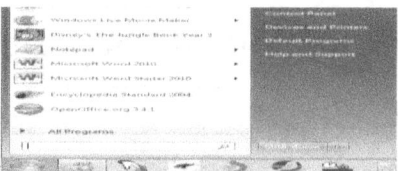

Click on <start> <control panel>

System and security

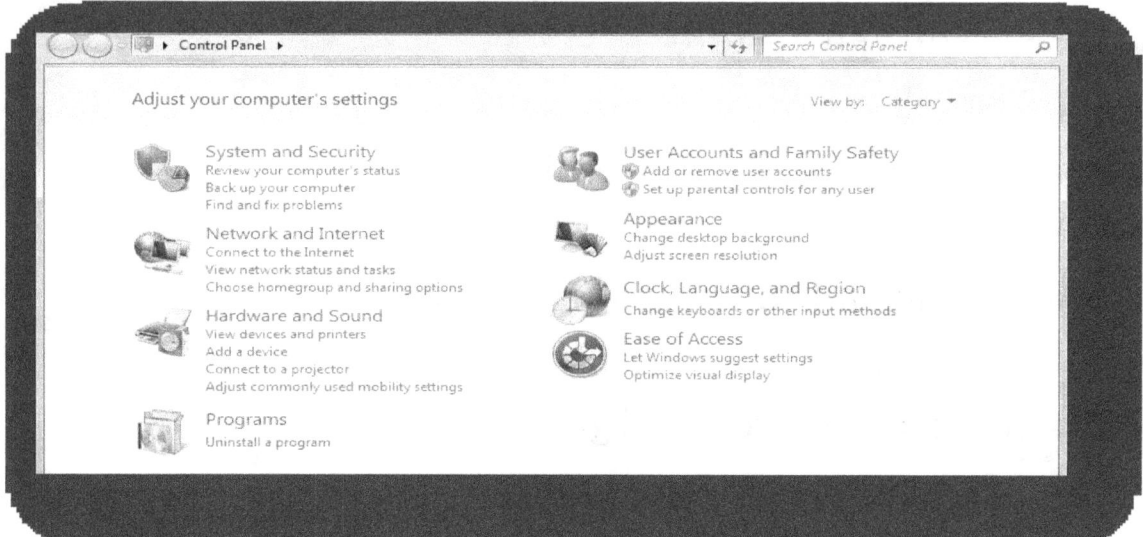

Windows update

Windows is automatically setup to download any updates that's available. The moment you connect to the internet, windows sneaks off and download updates.

The downloads are recommendable, however if you have limited download time available you can change the settings to have windows ask your permission to download files.

Change settings on updates:

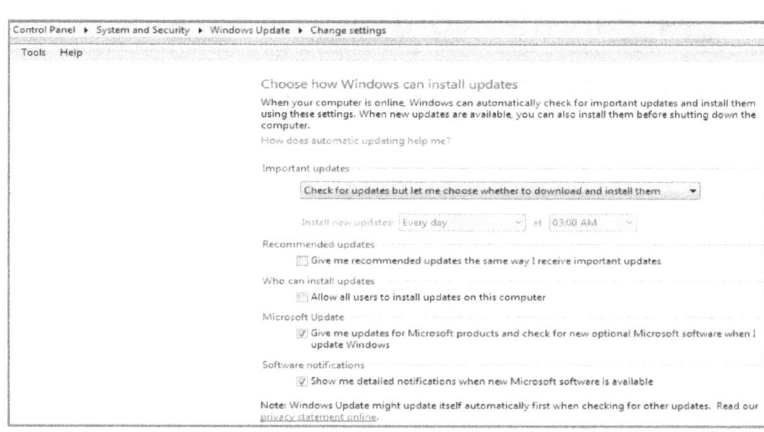

> ➤ Click on start
> ➤ Click on control panel
> ➤ Select system and security
> ➤ Select windows update
> ➤ Click on change settings
> ➤ Change automatic update to "let me choose to download and install updates

Action center

The action centre will inform you of any problems on your computer and request that you take action

A little flag will appear on the lower right side of your screen when you need to take action

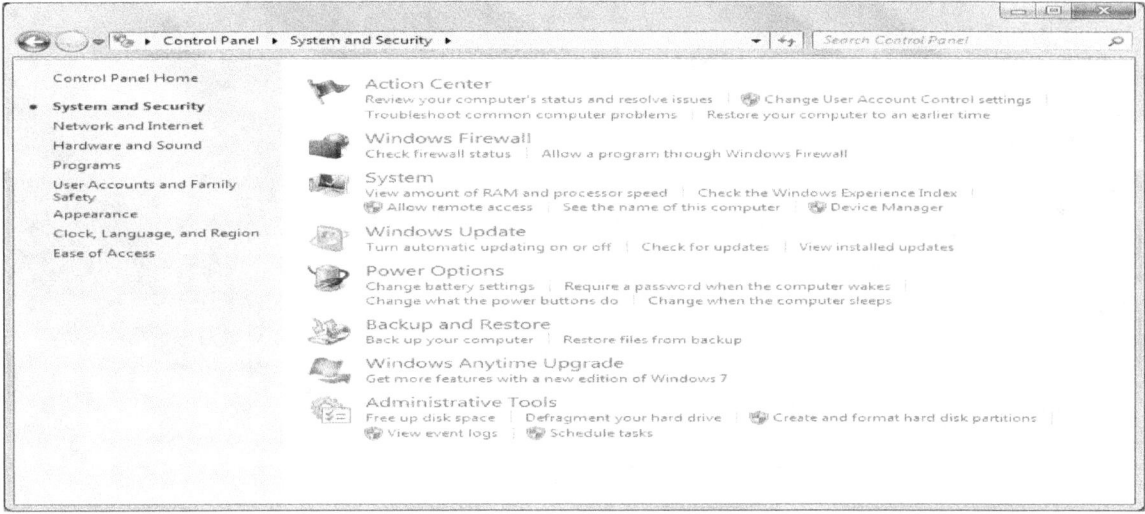

Firewall

A firewall is a special program that prevents hackers (other people) from gaining access to your computer and create damage or steal your information.

Windows 7 has included a special firewall protection against hackers,

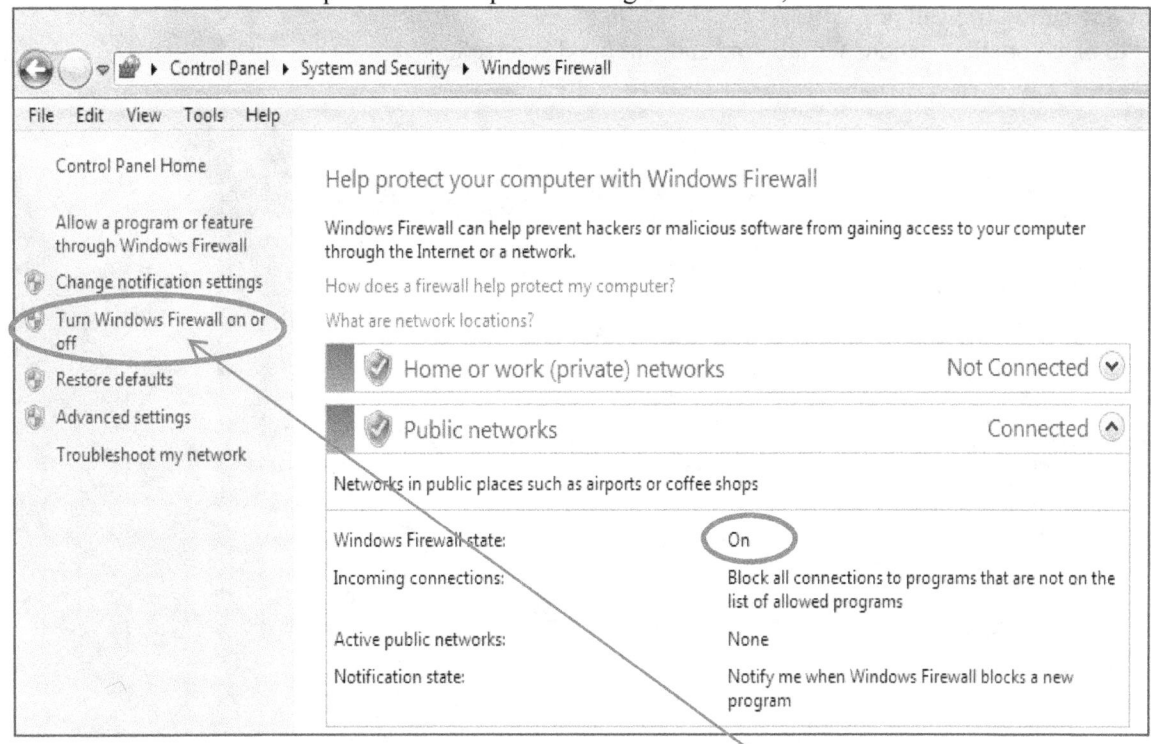

> Click on control panel, system security, turn windows firewall on

The following screen will appear where you can Change notification settings of the firewall

> Click inside the checkbox if you want to be notified when windows firewall blocks a program

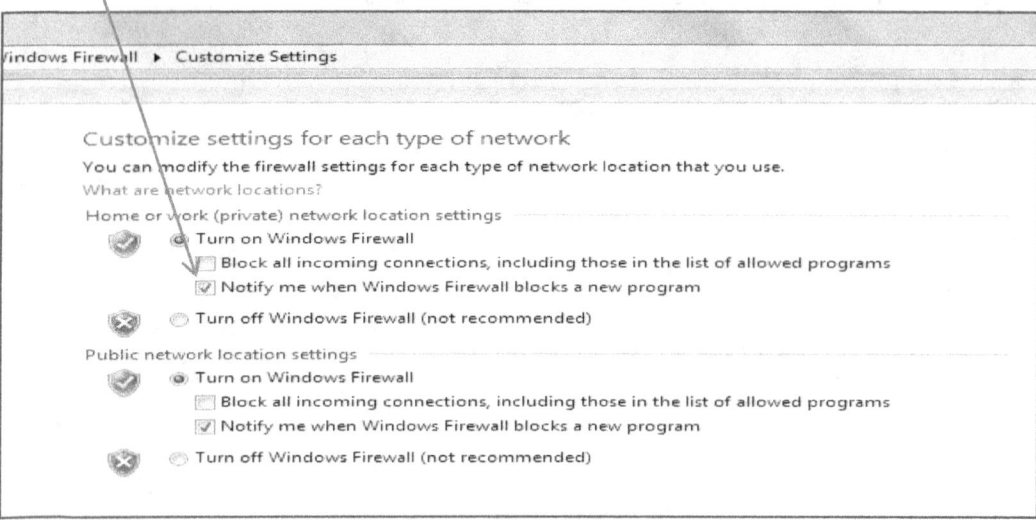

Advanced settings

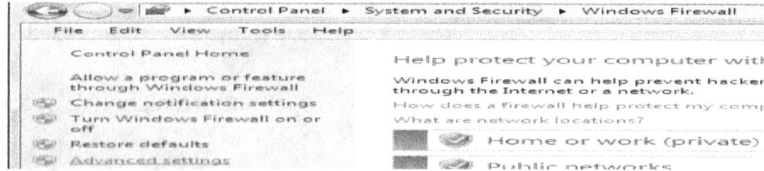

Click on Advance settings:

> Click on windows firewall properties
> Select to block or allow actions for inbound and outbound connections

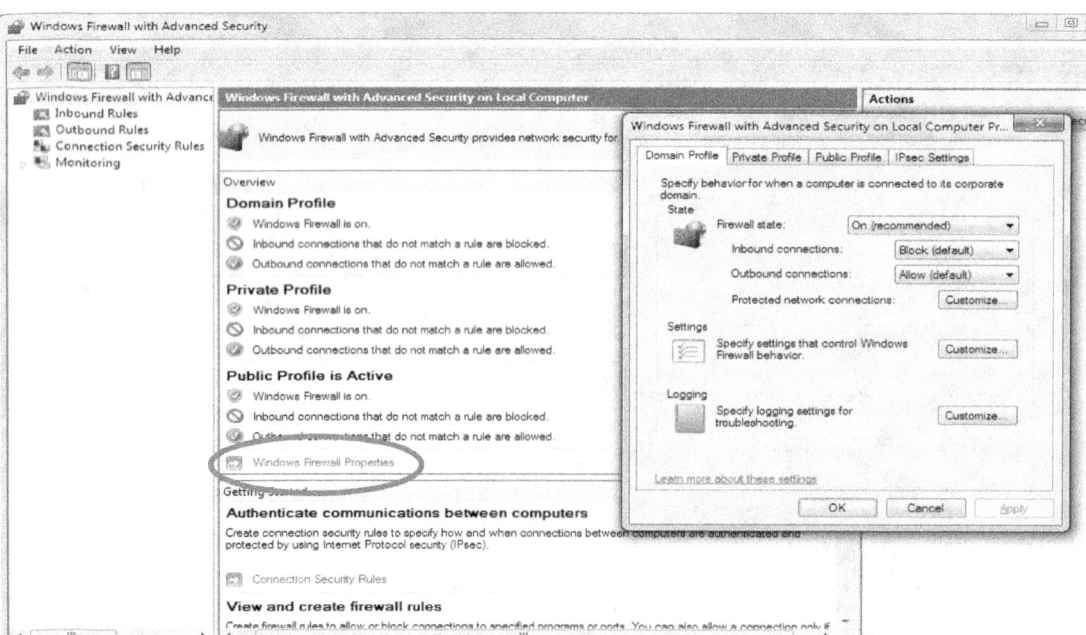

Using Windows firewall, you can allow programs through firewall.

Thus your computer will be protected from illegal internet access, and only the programs that you give permission will be allowed through the firewall

How to allow a program through the windows firewall:

➢ Click on control panel, system and security, Firewall
➢ Click on allow another program,(located at the left top of the screen)
➢ and select the program from the list that you want to allow through the firewall
by clicking inside the checkbox(little square). The following symbol will appear,√ this indicated that program on the left side that is on the same line, will be allowed through the firewall.
To deactivate this program, just click inside the checkbox again, and the symbol will disappear, indicating that the program will no longer be allowed through the firewall.
Thus when there is a little white square next to the program name it indicates that this program will not be allowed through the firewall, only when there is a symbol inside the little square will the program be allowed through the firewall.

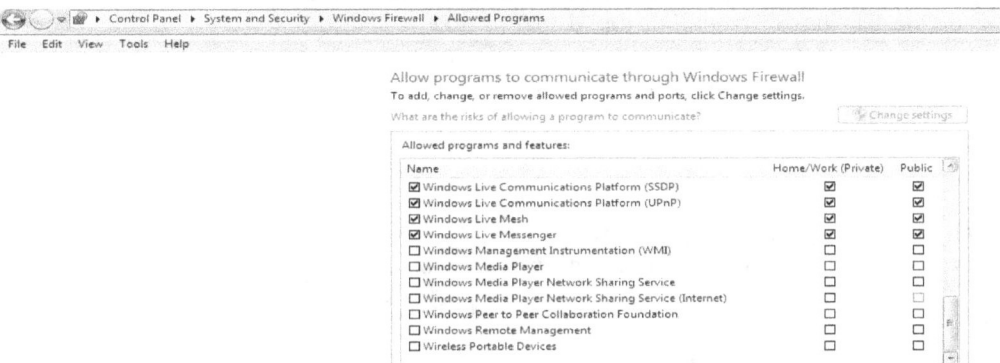

System

➢ Click on control panel, system and security, system

When selecting system you will be able to view the capacity of the RAM and processing speed of the computer.

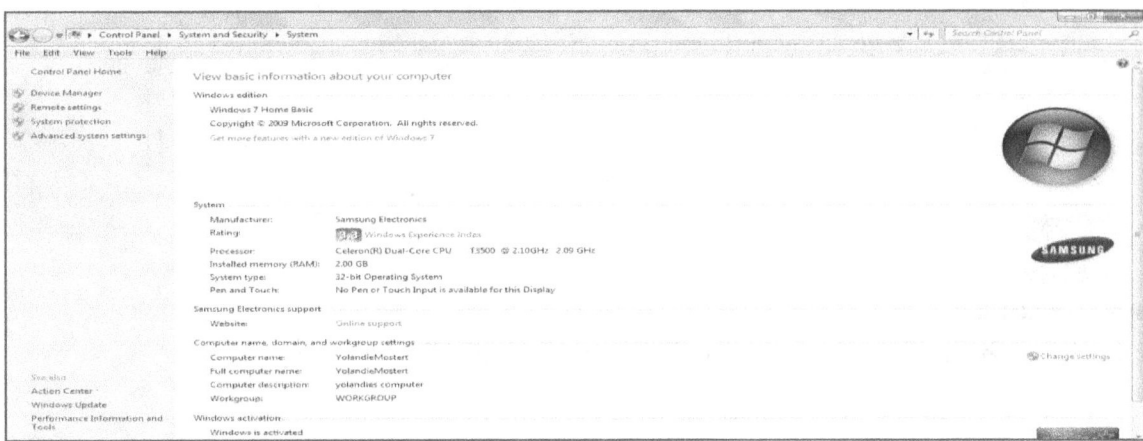

You will also be able to activate remote assistance

Remote assistance

Is a program that will allow someone else to work on your computer that is connected to a network

➤ Click on Control panel, System and security, system, remote assistance

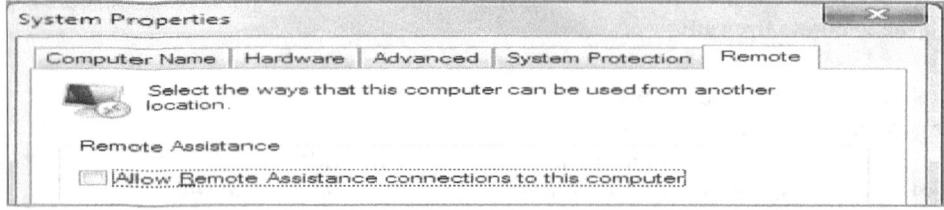

Backup and restore

Your computer is scheduled to make backup copies of your computer every seven days at a certain time, you can use this backup to restore your computer if something goes wrong. You can also change the schedule so that it backs up the data at a different time and date.

➤ Click on, Control panel, System security, Backup your computer

System image

A system image is a copy of the drives required to run windows.
A system image can be used to restore your computer if it doesn't want to work.

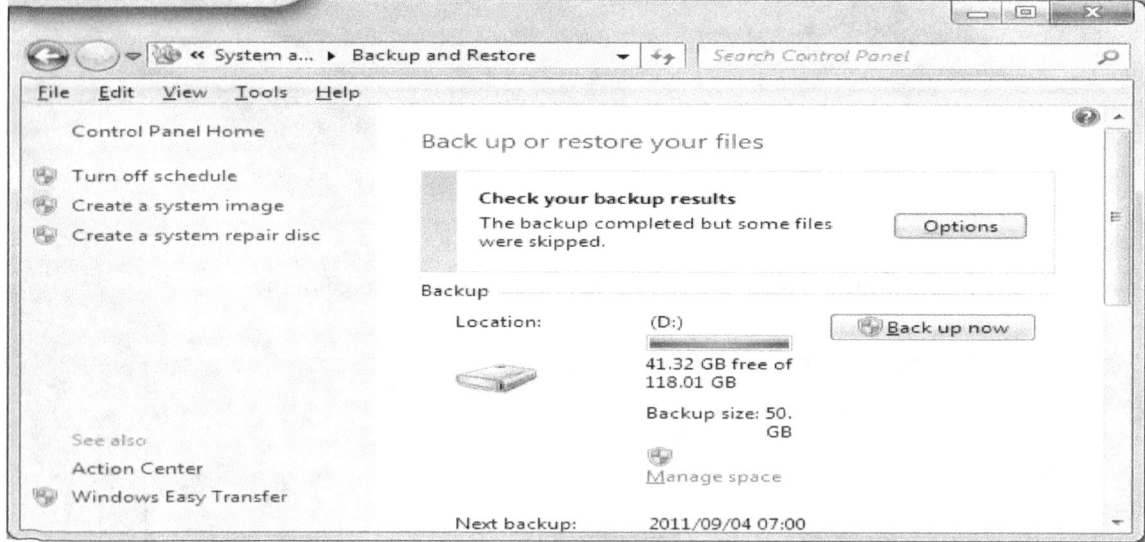

Restoring a system

➤ Click on, Start, control panel, system and security, start and fix problems, recovery

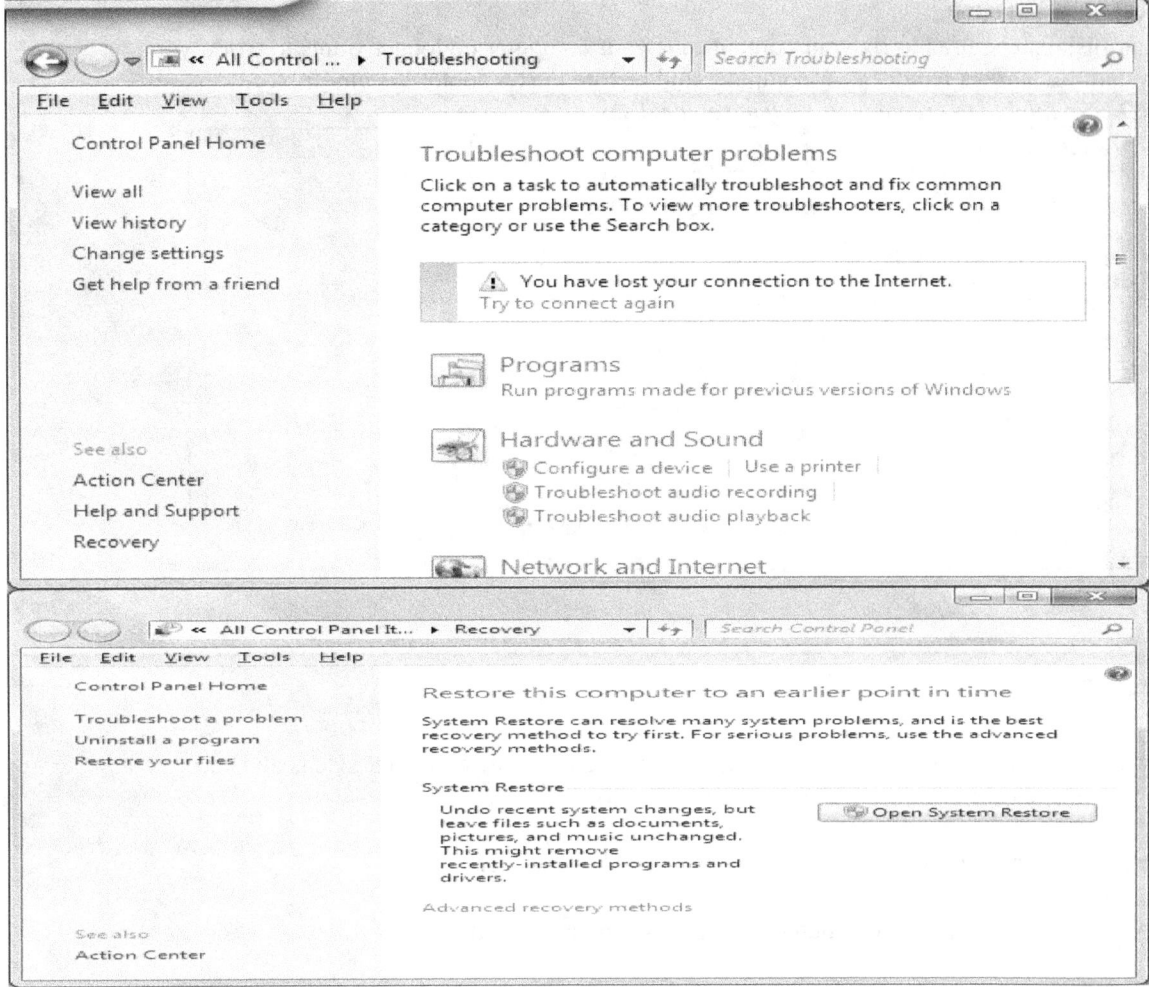

➤ Click on restore your files

System restore.

There can be many backups made every month. You can choose which backup you want to restore

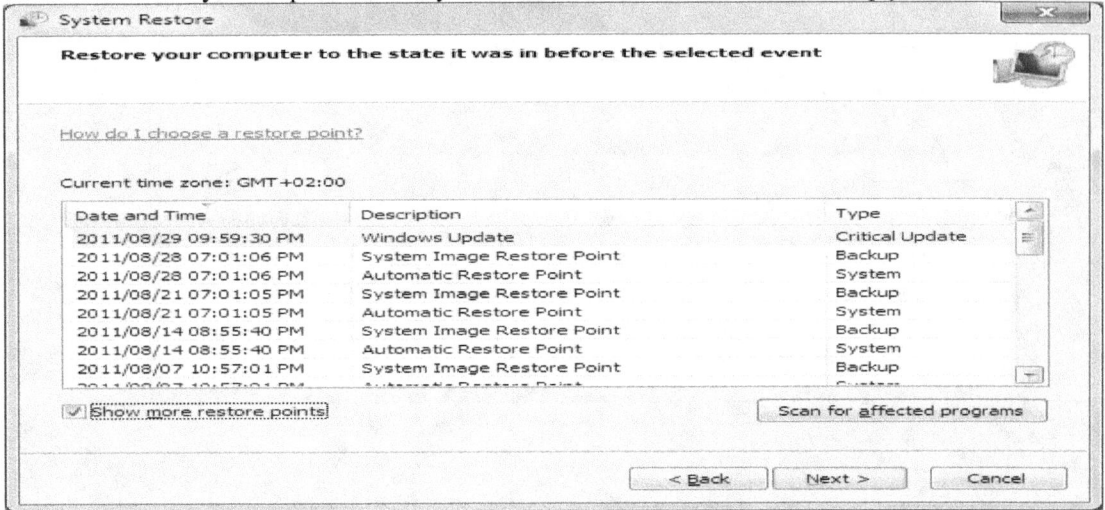

Creating a system repair disk.

A system repair disk can be used to fix your computer. If your computer no longer wants to work, you can use the system repair disk to boot your computer and restore the computer system image.

Have clean CD''s available to create your system repair disks.

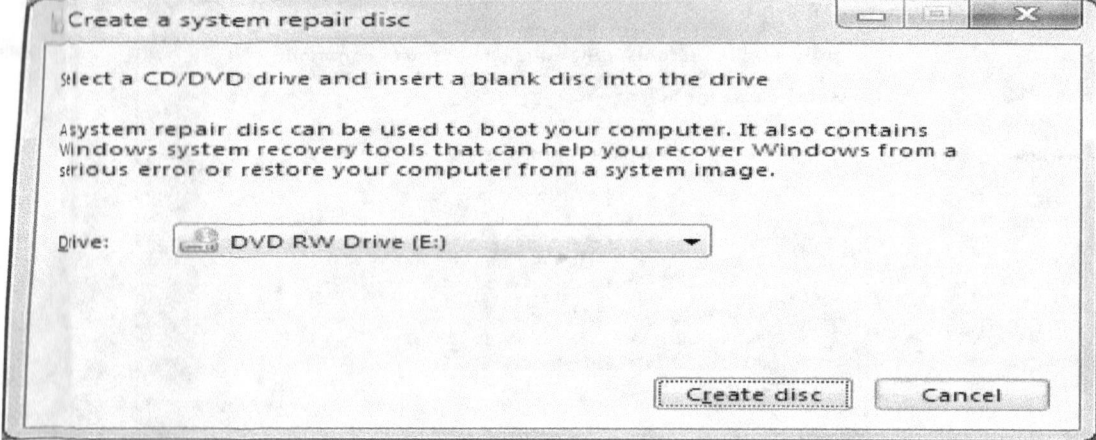

Power options

With power options you can change the battery options, change when the computer sleeps and add passwords to your system.

With power plan you can setup settings that saves power and battery life.

You can choose when and how your computer will go to sleep or hibernate.

Sleep will keep documents in memory so that you can quickly access them again

Hibernation will keep the documents on your hard disk and switch off the computer

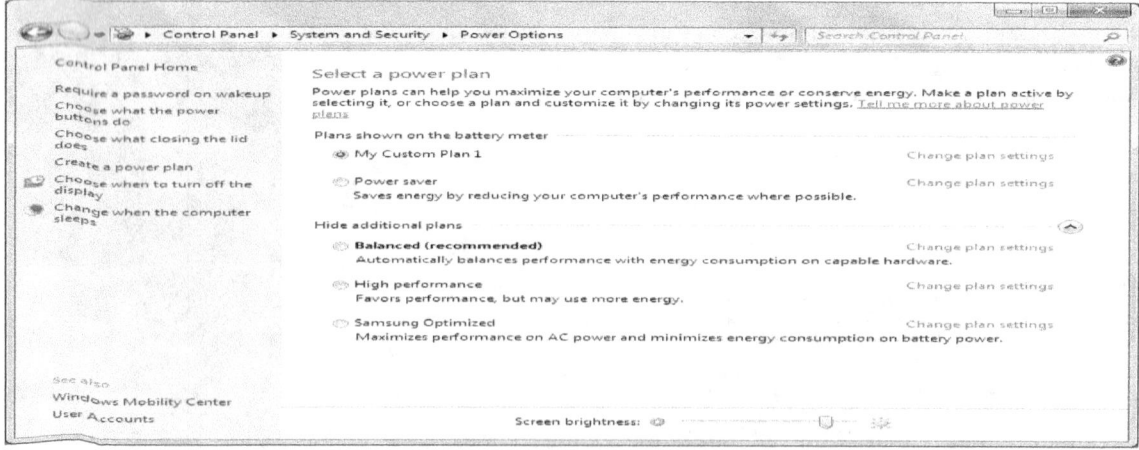

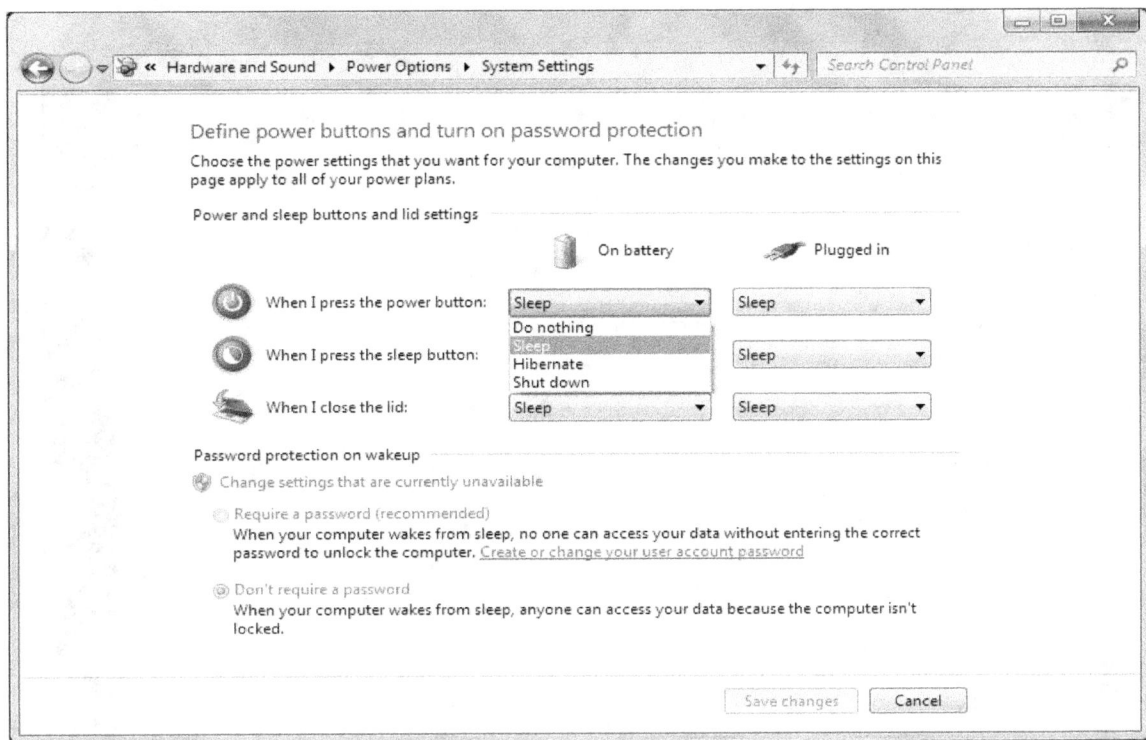

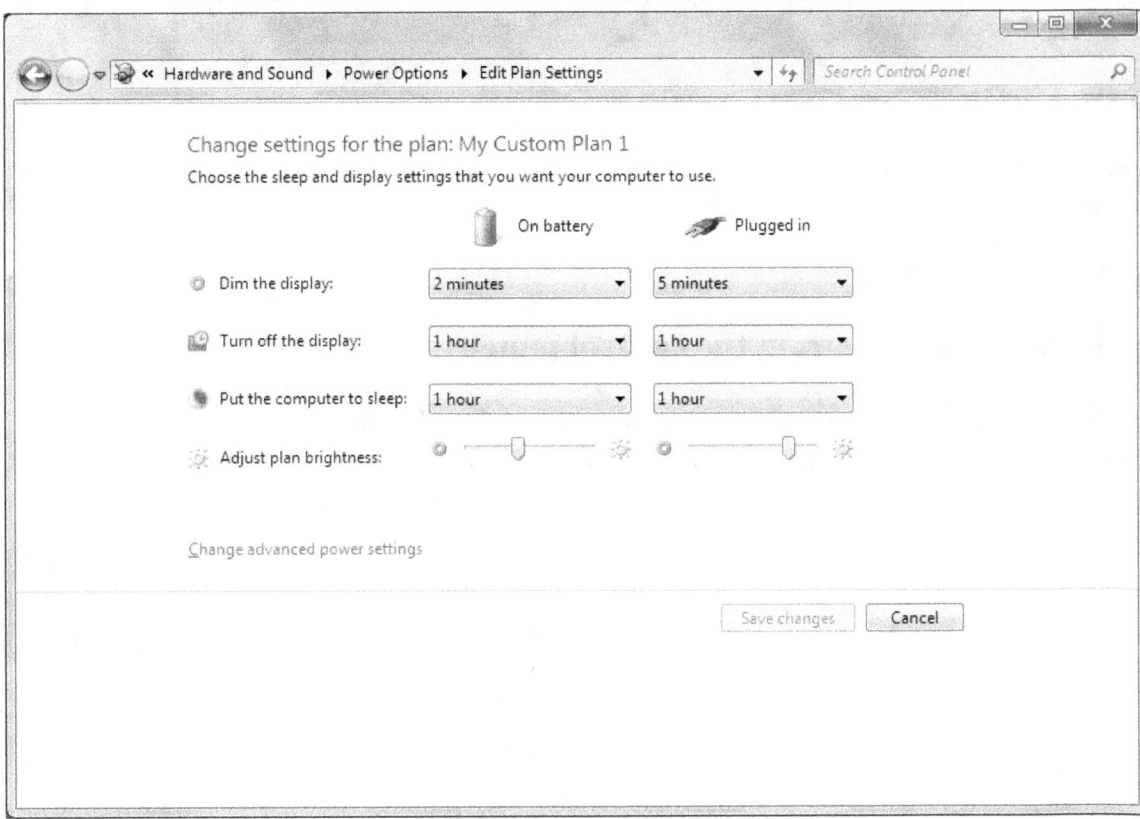

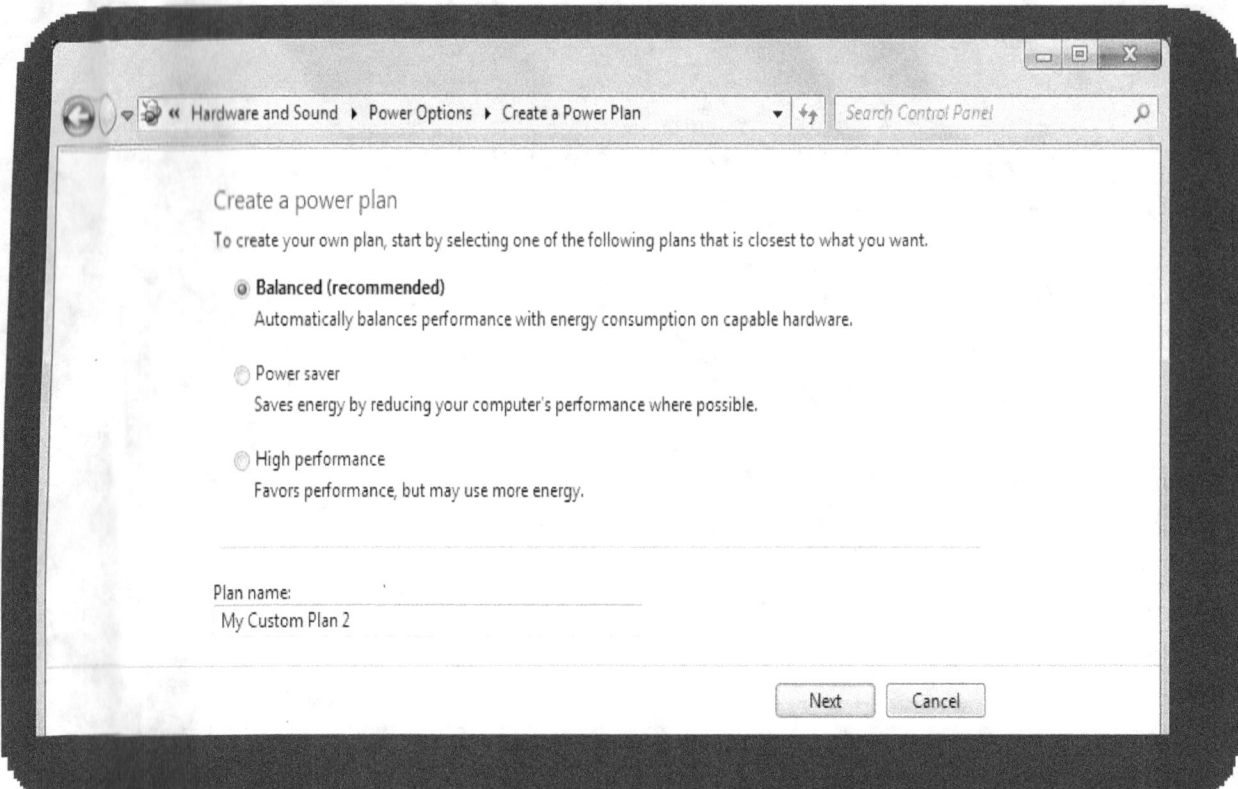

Administrative tools

With administrative tools you can Free up disk space, create and format hard disk partitions, **Defragment a disk**

Defragmentation will make your computer work faster

Activating defragmentation from the control panel

➢ Click on control panel, security and settings, administrative tools, defragment

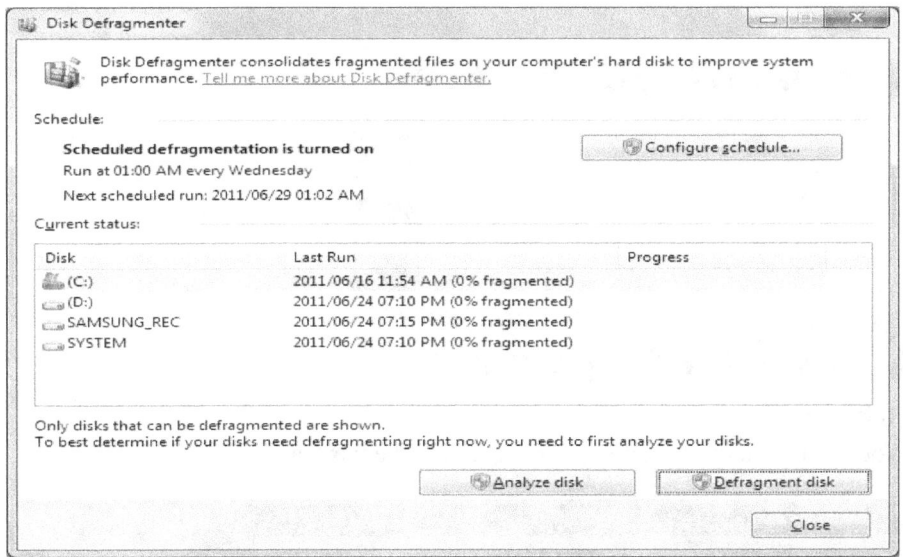

You can schedule to run defragmentation, daily weekly or monthly or you can do it manually.

You may analyse the disk first, if you like, to check if it is necessary to defragment the disk

Running defragment from windows explorer

> Right click on C drive and select properties, click on tools

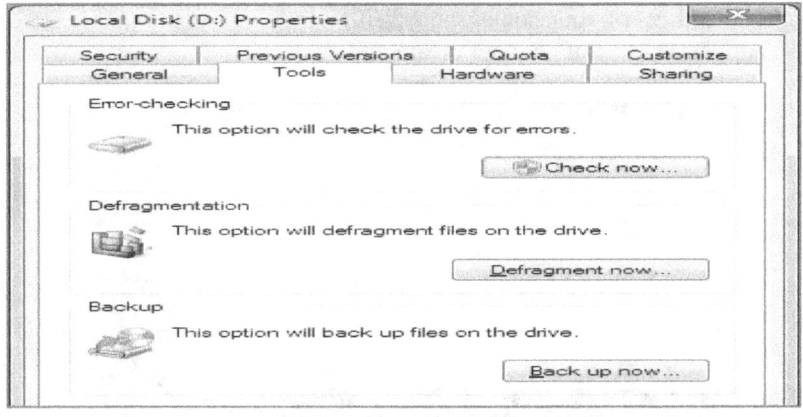

Network and internet

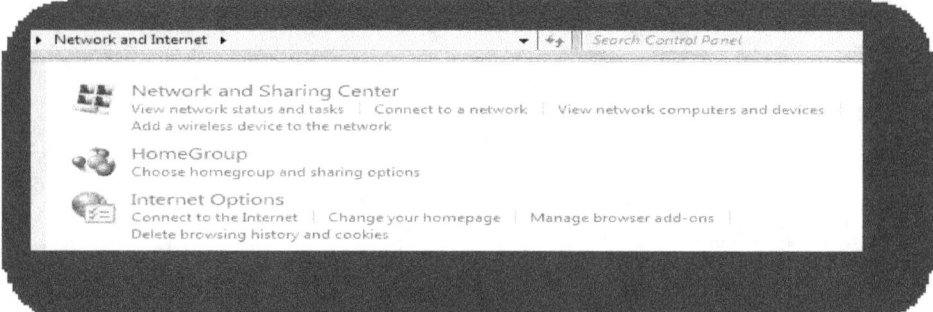

Network and sharing center

Network and sharing center allows you to view network status and connect to a network and add a wireless device to a network

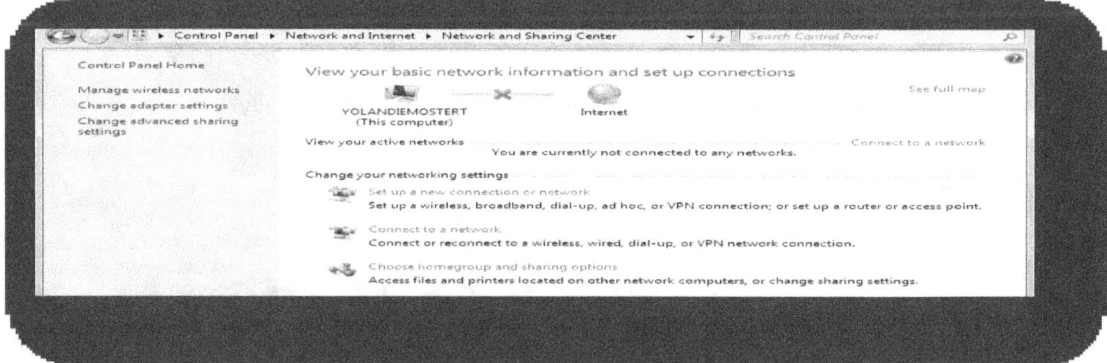

Homegroup

You can choose what to share with other members of your homegroup. With windows 7 starter,home or basic version you can join a homegroup, however you may not create one.

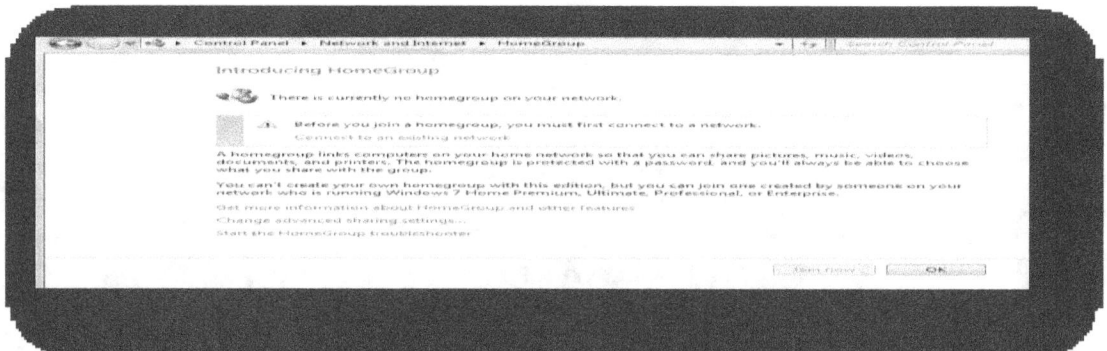

Internet options

With internet options you can change all the settings for your internet connection, for example you can setup security settings to disable cookies on your computer

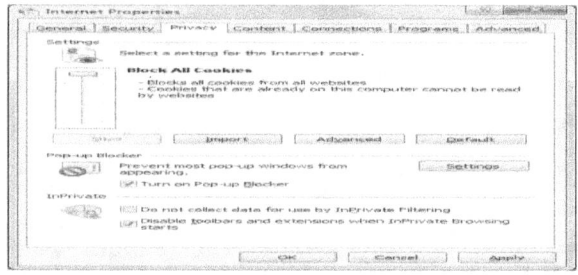

> ➢ Click on start,control panel,Network and internet, delete cookies,
> ➢ Click on privacy. Slide the bar to the top if you want to block all cookies,
> ➢ slide it down if you want to allow cookies

Blue tooth file transfer and internet connection

If your phone have blue tooth functionality you can transfer files to and from your pc and use your phones internet facilities on your pc.

The blue tooth connection are usualy located at the right bottom of the taskbar next to the date and time, you should find a small white up arrow, click on it to reveal functions

➢ Double click on blue tooth

The bluetooth function will reveal   devices that are available

Ensure tht your cellphone is switched on and that bluetooth is on and pairing has been activated.

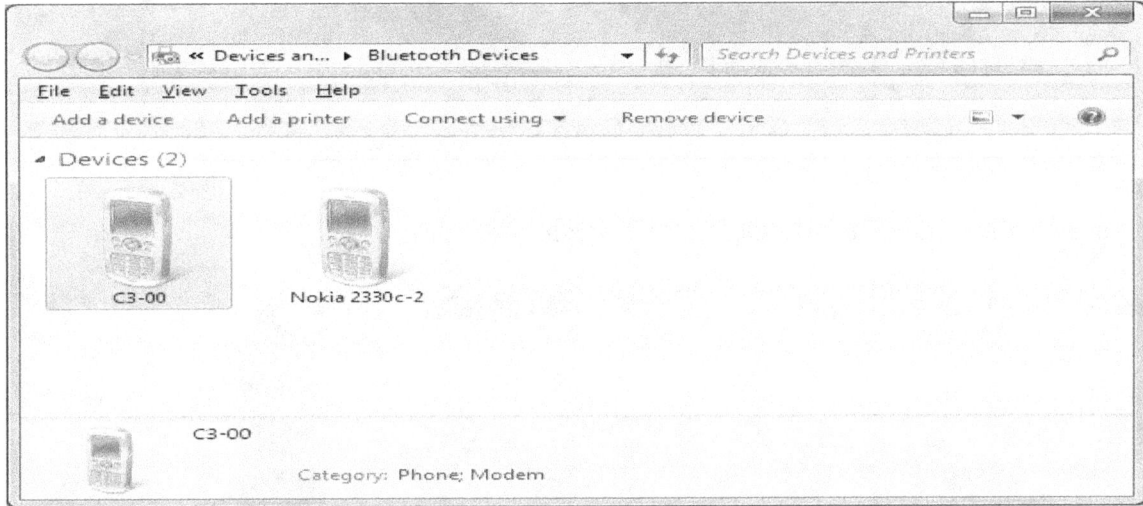

+ Double click on the device that you wish to use, the following screen should appear
+ To connect to the internet, click on connect
+ To transfer files from your sel phone to your pc, click on File Transfer

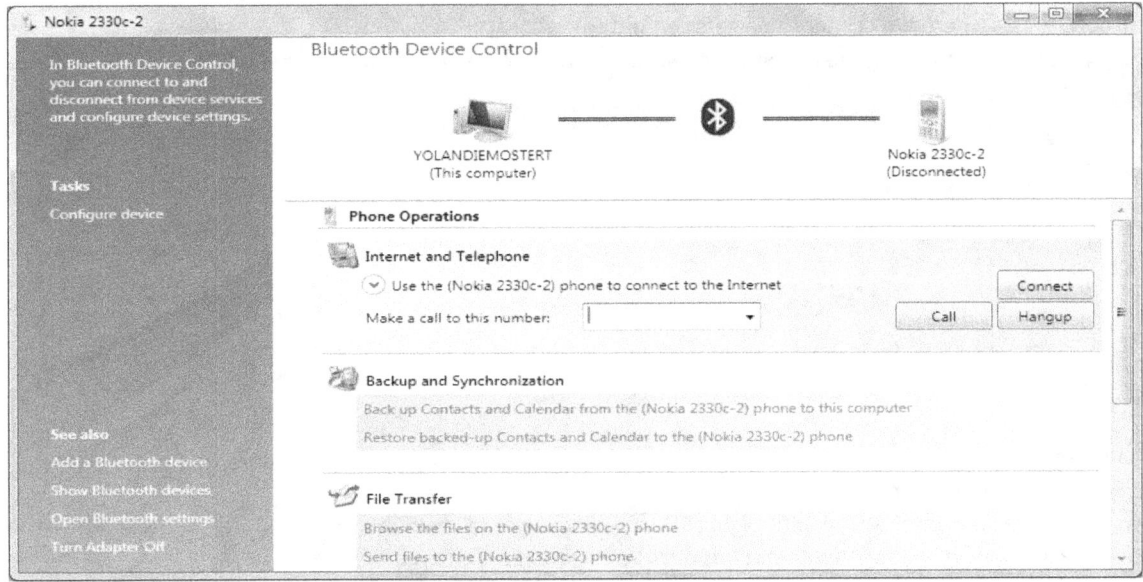

Hardware and sound

With this option you can add new devices for example printers ,scanners,cameras

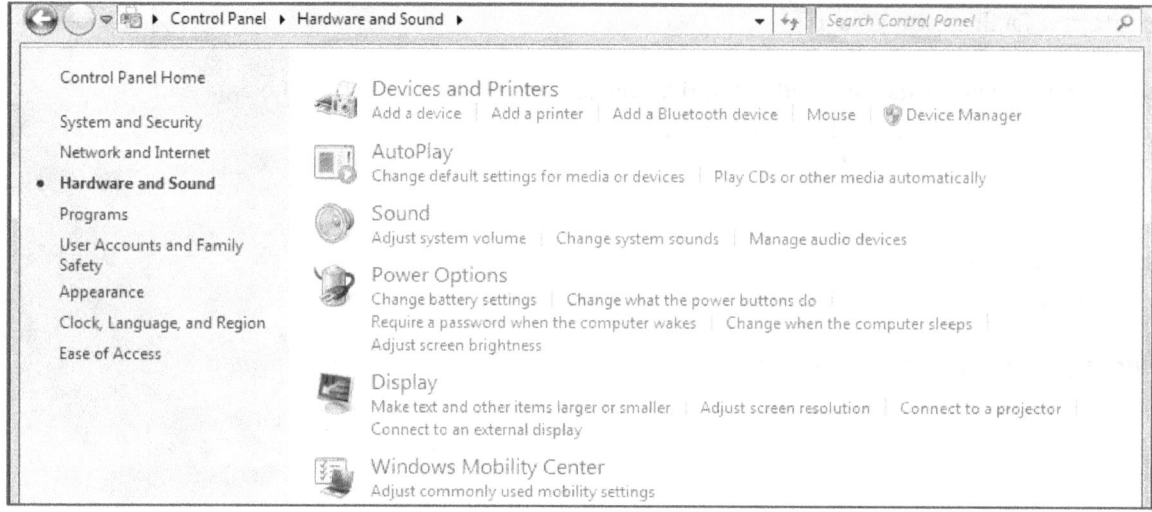

Add a printer

Specify first whether you are connecting a local printer or a network printer

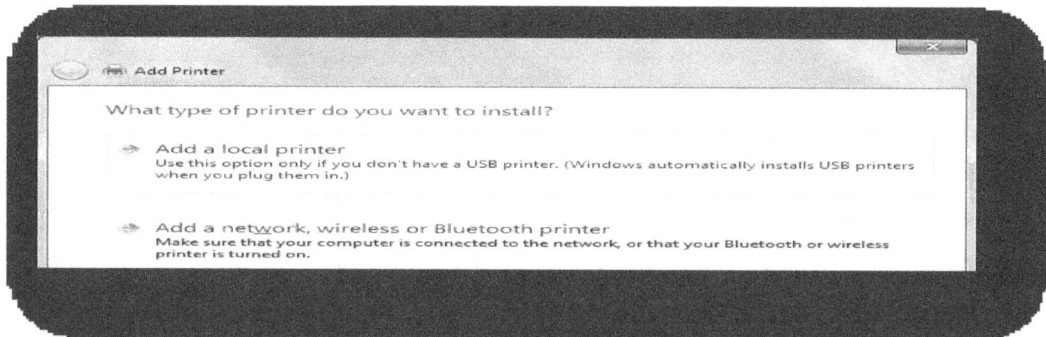

> Select a port (this is where the printer cable gets connected)
> Select a printer driver (choosing the wrong driver will cause your printer not to work correctly)

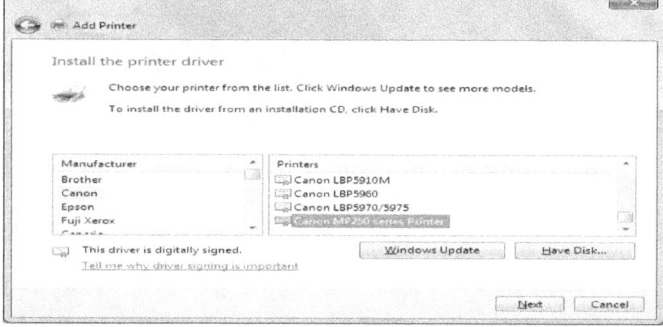

Selecting a default printer
> Click on start, devices and printers
> Click on the printer you want to print with, right click and choose <set as default printer>
> *A green circle will appear on the printer that has been selected to be the default printer*

Autoplay

Sometimes when you insert a cd into a computer it immediately starts
You can choose what happens when you insert each type of media device:

Sound

With the sound option you can change the volume and settings of the sound
Adjust system volume
➢ Drag the bar up or down to change the volume of the sound

Automatically adjusting the sound when you have an incoming call
➢ Change system sound, click on communication

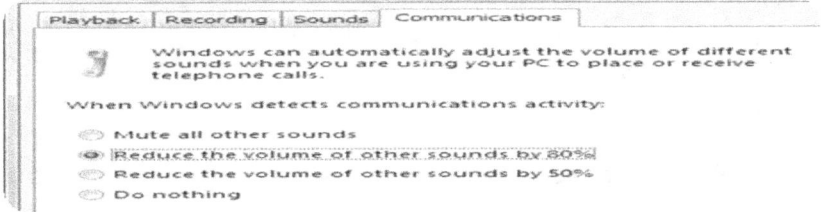

Windows mobility centre

The most commonly used laptop settings are available here for you to change.

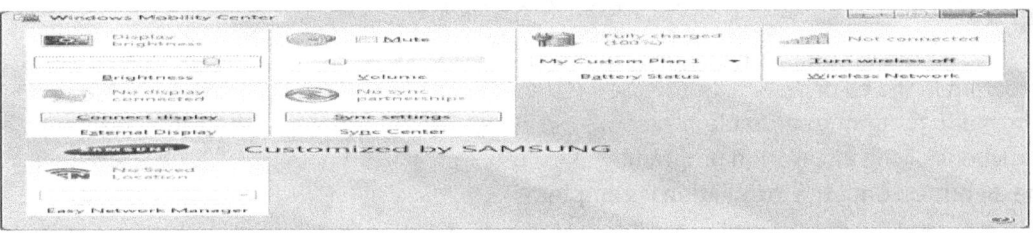

Programs

You can remove programs with this option and set default settings and add gadgets to your computer

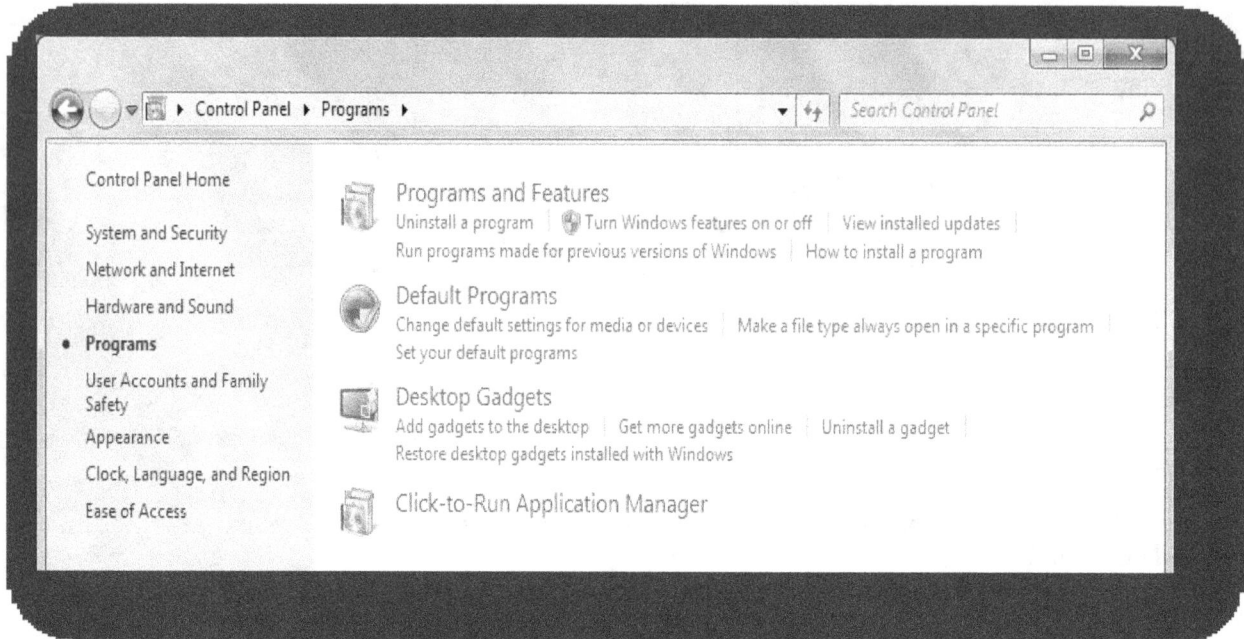

Uninstall a program

When you no longer use a program it is better to uninstall it, since the program files takes up space on your hard disk

- ➢ Click on uninstall program
- ➢ Select from a list which program you wish to uninstall

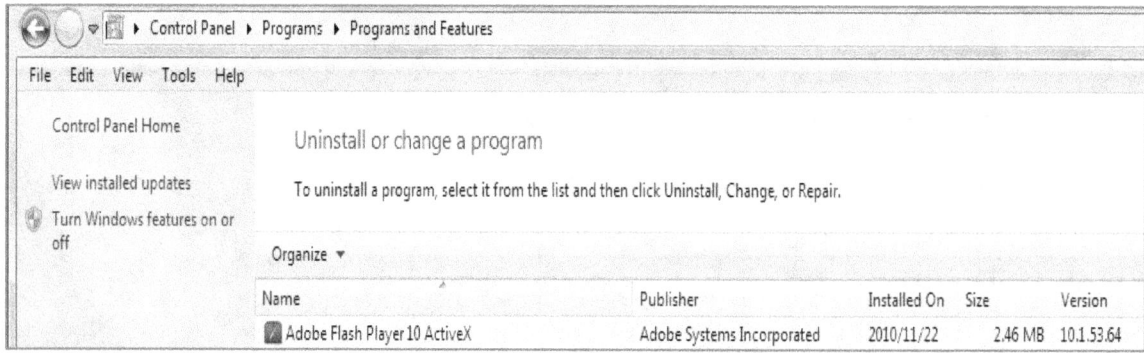

Installing a program

- ➢ Put the new program in the cd drive
- ➢ A request will be made to run the setup file
- ➢ Follow the instructions of the installation program
- ➢ Click on the <next> button until the installation is complete

Clock language and region

You can change the date time, location and number formatting

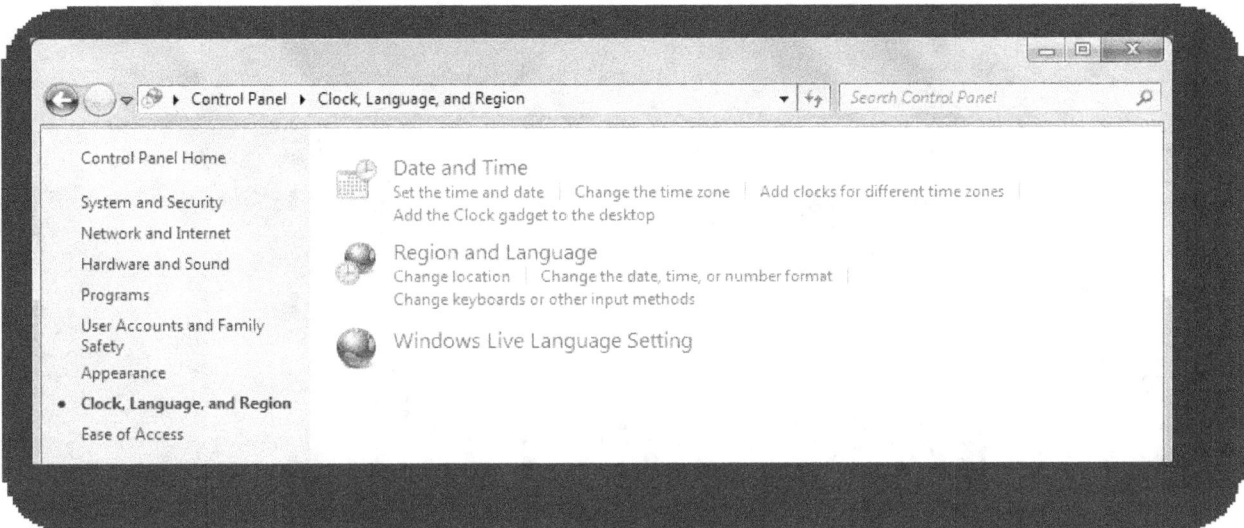

Date and time

You can setup more than one clock

> Click on add clock for different time zones

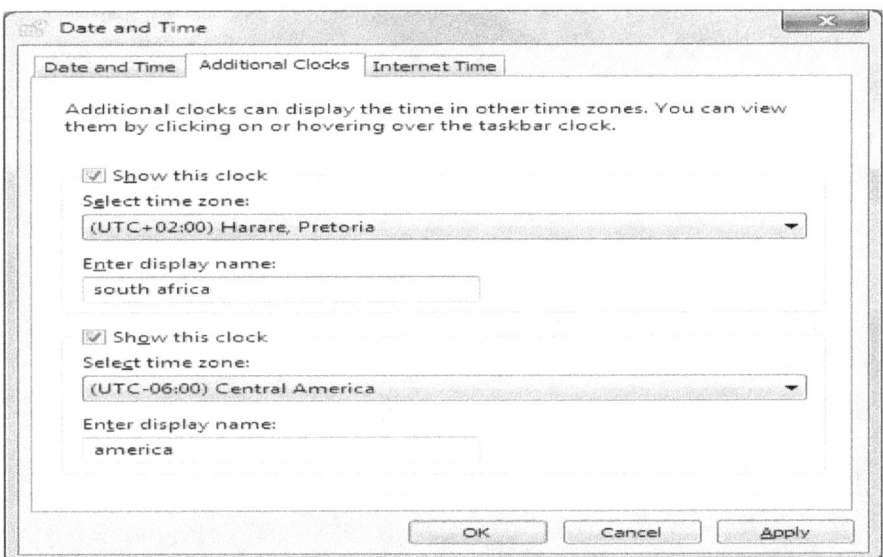

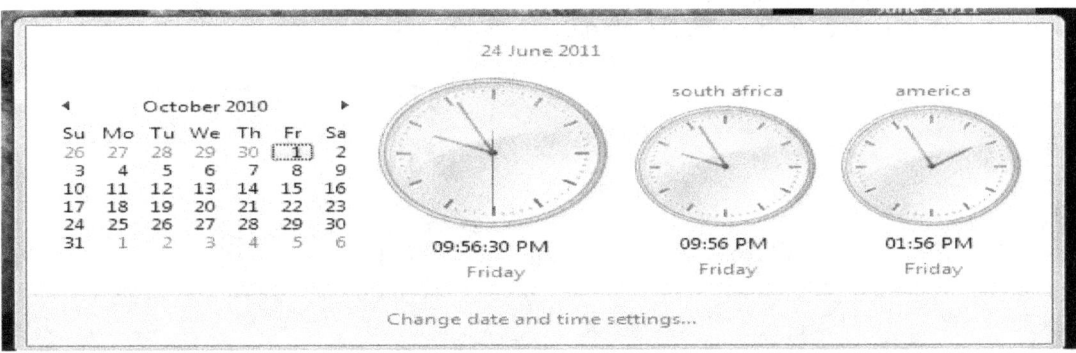

Region and language

> ➢ Click on Start, Control panel, Clock language and region Change date time or number format, Additional settings

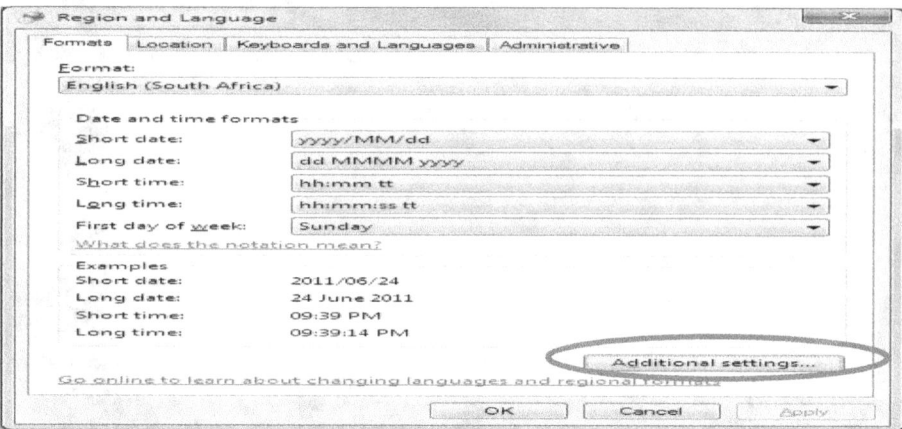

> ➢ Click on additional settings

You can change the decimal symbol, default decimal spaces and negative number formatting

> ➢ Click on the down arrow to make changes or type in the new format

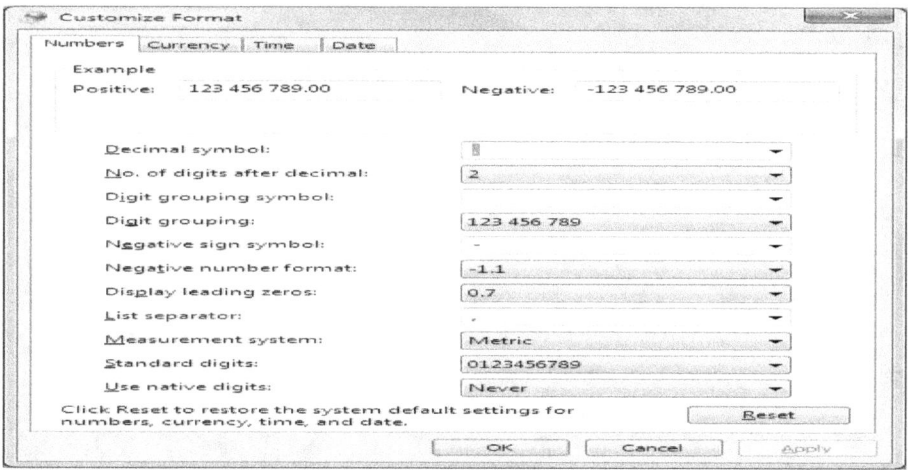

Currency
To change the currency you must select the currency tab
To change the R to a $, click inside the currency symbol rectangle and type in $

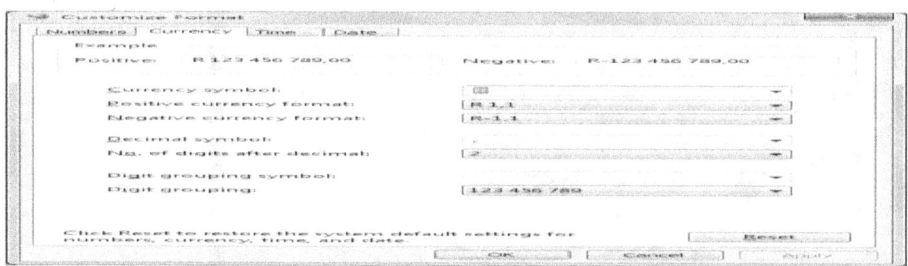

Change how your mouse works

You can make the arrow bigger by selecting a different option

How to change the mouse pointer

➢ Click on start, Control panel, ease of access, change how your mouse works

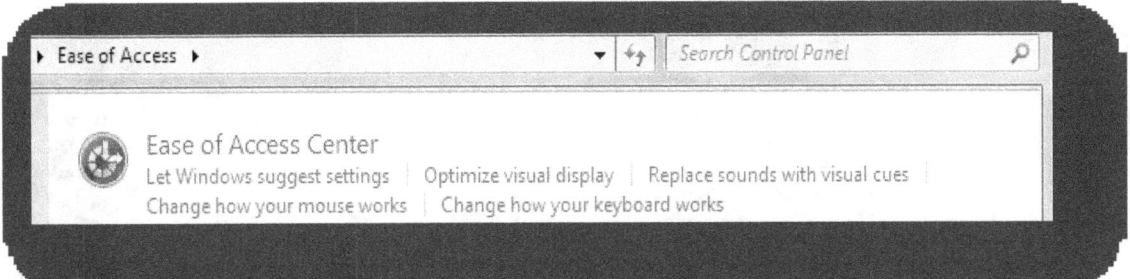

The following screen will appear: Click inside the little round circle next to the option of your choice.

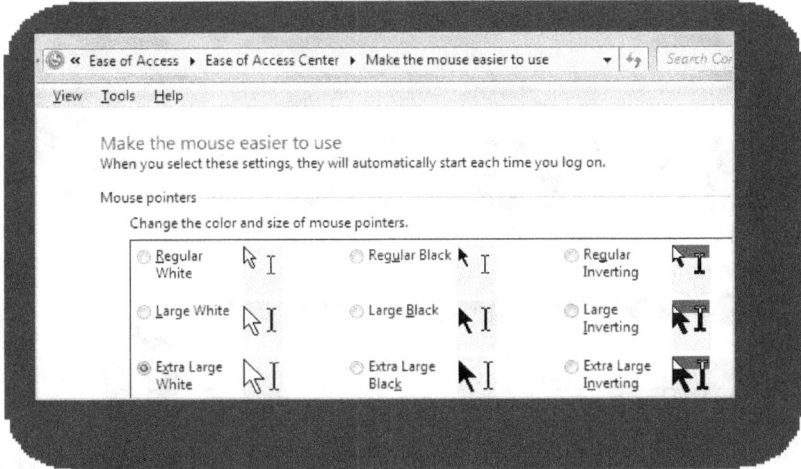

To change other mouse settings
➢ Click on Start, Control panel, hardware and sound, mouse
You can change the primary and secondary click of the mouse buttons by selecting left handed or right handed will switch the buttons. You can also change the appearance of the mouse cursor for certain actions

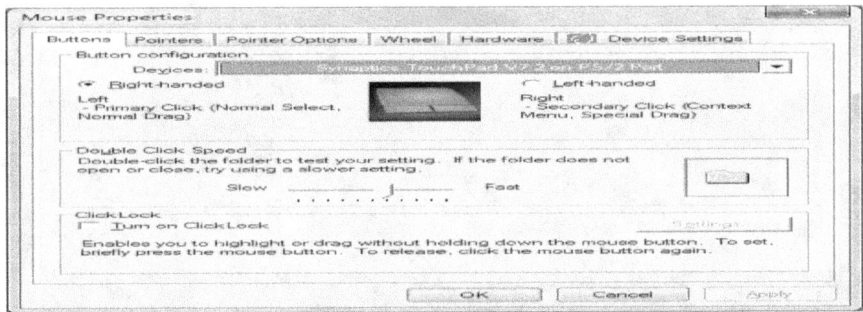

Changing the appearance on your screen

➢ Click on start, control panel ,appearance
➢ Select display

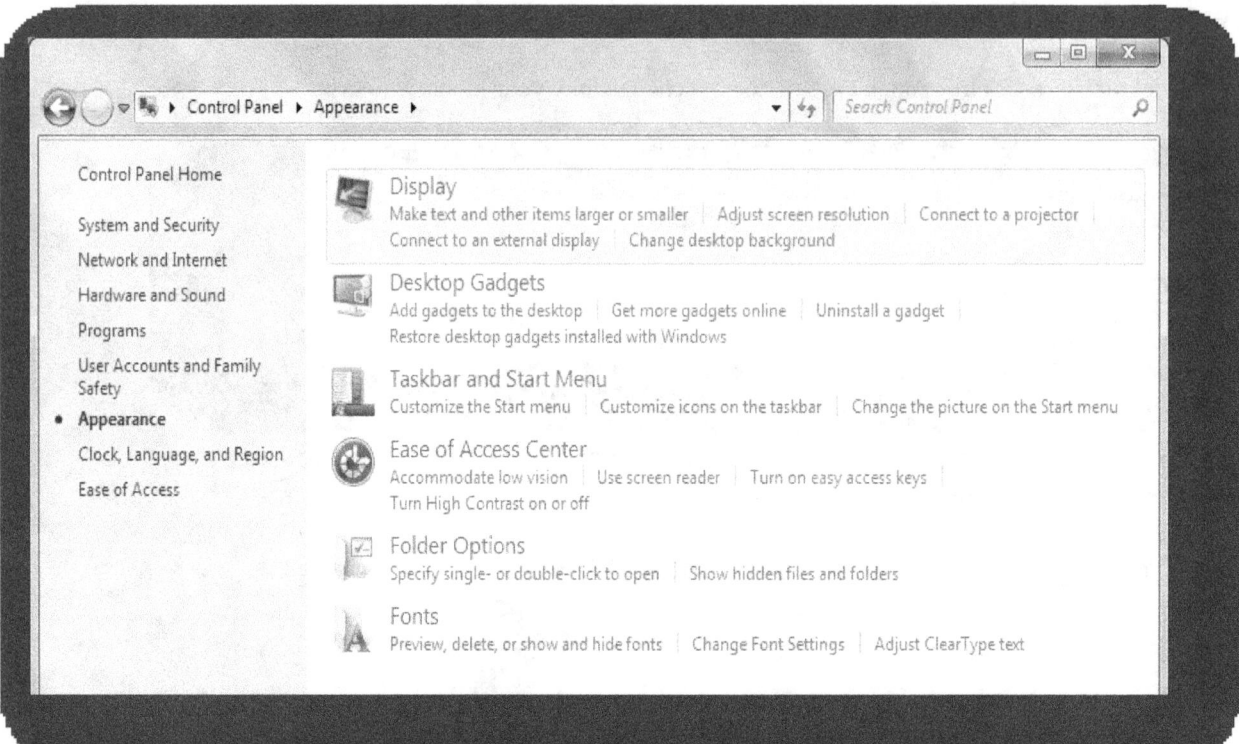

The blue dot indicates which action is activated; you can choose small or medium size text, to change to medium size text click inside the small round circle to make the action active.

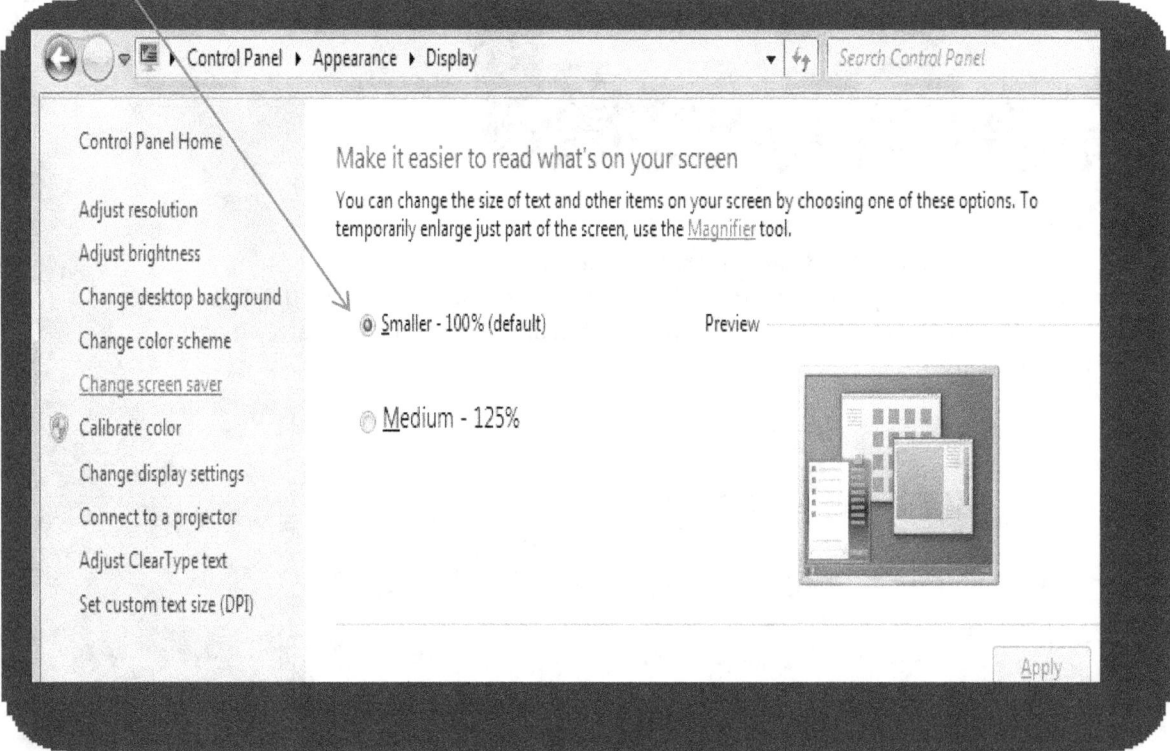

Screen saver

> ➢ **Click on Control panel, Appearance, Display,**
> ➢ **Click on <change screen saver, located on the left side of the screen**

A screen saver is a picture icon or words that are moving on the screen. When the time has elapsed, the screen saver will start. You can type in the amount of time before the screen saver will start.

When you stop working on your computer, the screen saver will be activated. If for example you haven't worked on your pc for 8 minutes and you haven't touched your computer then the screen saver will start if you have set the time for 8 minutes.

Click on change screen saver, next to the word <wait> there is a number. Change the number to wait for 8 minutes, you can press the up or down arrows or you can type in the number.

Change desktop background

The desktop background is the picture that you see in the background when your computer start. You can add a picture of your family to the desktop
- Click on the browse button and select your own picture or select an item that is available.
- Click on the down arrow to choose from a list

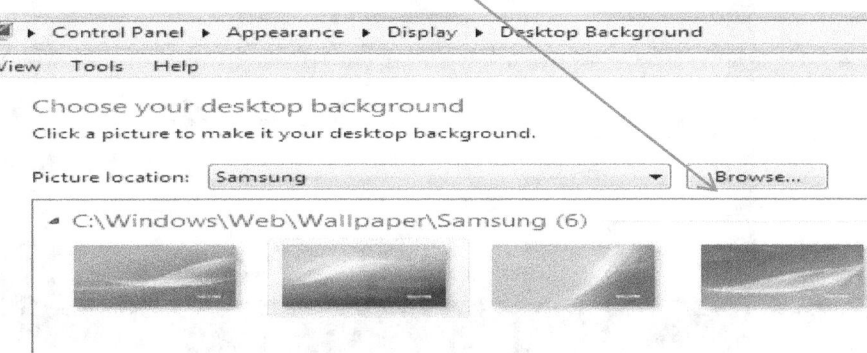

Creating a user account

A user account is a special log in screen that you can create for any user.

The specific user account will have its own profile and information on the start menu and shortcuts to the desktop will be stored for this user.

Access to the computer will be specified whereby some users will have more access to the computer and others will have fewer privileges.

How to create a user account

➤ Click on start, control panel, user account

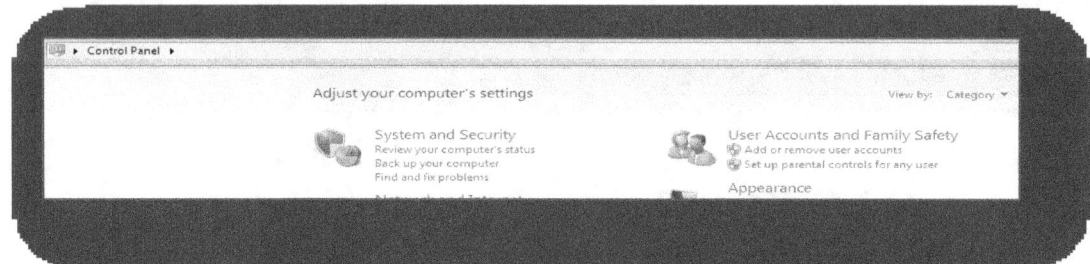

When you click on <add or remove user account, the account dialog box will appear showing all the current users.

➤ Click on <create a new account>

You can decide whether it will be a standard user that have restricted permissions or an administrative user that can install programs and change any setting on the computer.

Type in the name of the user and select whether it will have full access by clicking on administrative rights or limited access by clicking on standard user.

Click inside the round circle, which is called the radio button. A blue dot inside the radio button indicates the active choice. Click on <Create Account>

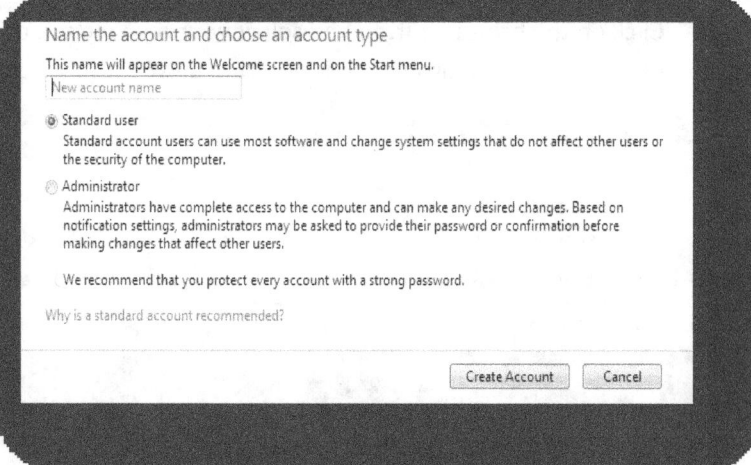

Parental control

With parental control, you can allow children, only specific time limits and control which programs they have access to.

> ➤ Click on Control Panel,User Accounts, Parental Controls,Click on one of the user accounts
>   The following screen will appear where you can control user access:

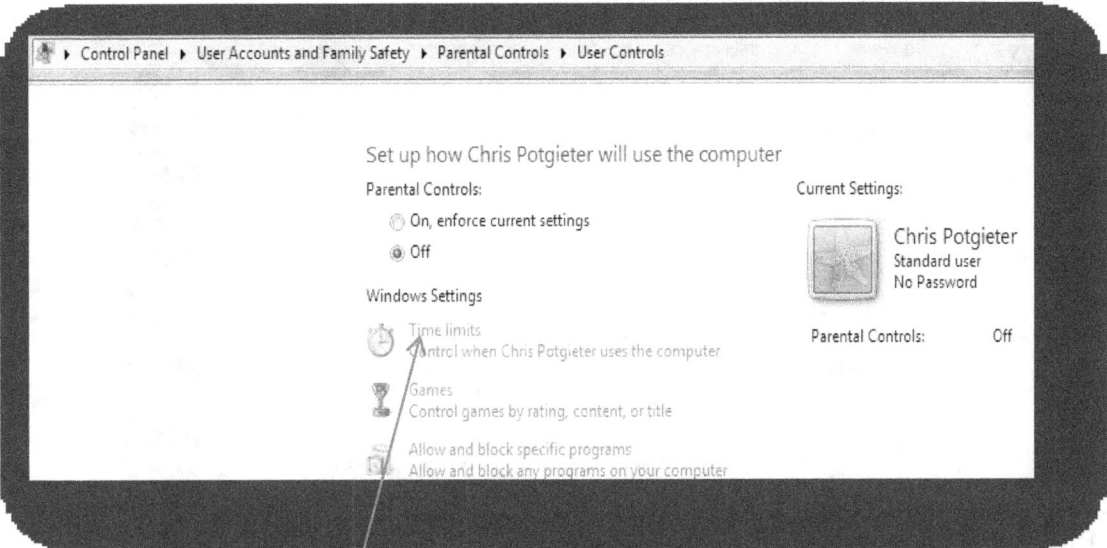

Time allocation table

You can specify what time the user is allowed to work on the computer

> ➤ Click on Time limits
> ➤ Click inside the blocks that you want to block. *The block will turn blue, and your child's face too*
>   The blue areas will not be accessible to this user
>   In the example below this user will not have access to the PC between 8pm and 6 am

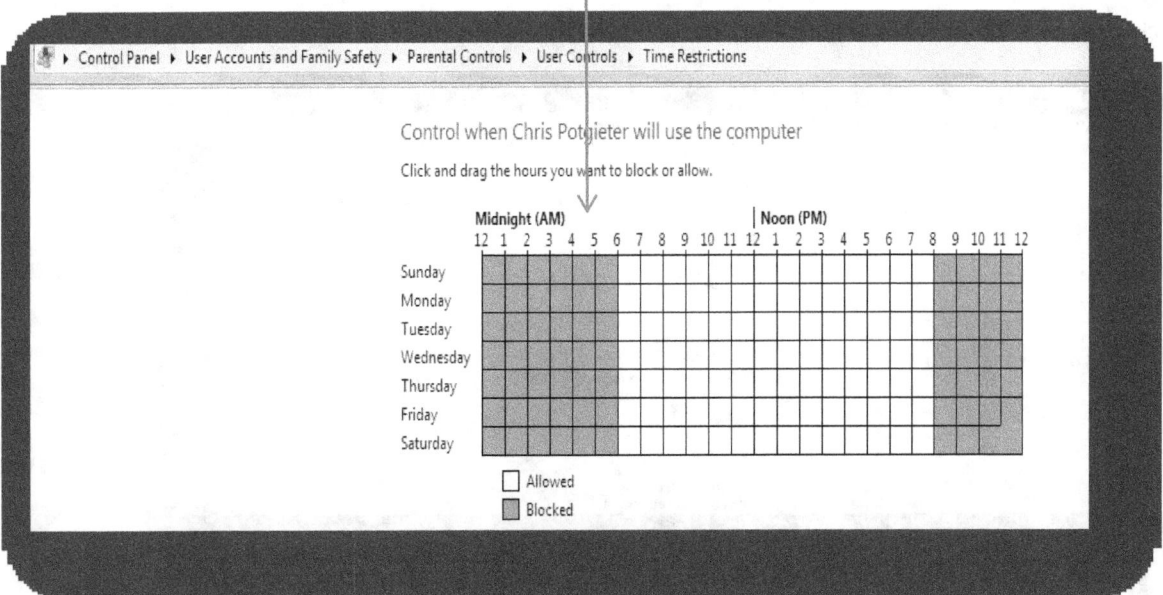

Blocking of programs

You can specify which programs the user is allowed to use

> ➤ Click inside the little round circle to specify if the user is allowed to use all programs or only programs that you specify
>
> ➤ Click inside the checkbox to allow access to a program. An √ inside the little square on the left means that this user is allowed access to this program

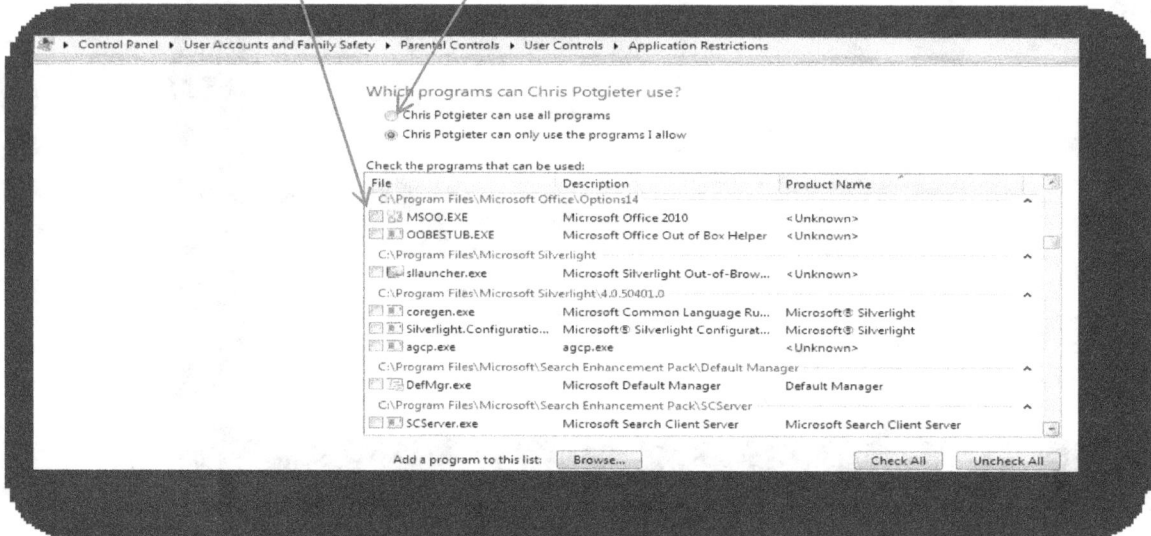

Games

Specify if user is allowed to play games, by clicking inside the little round circle next to <yes> or <no>

You can also specify what games the user is allowed to play

> ➤ Click on games, allow or block specific games

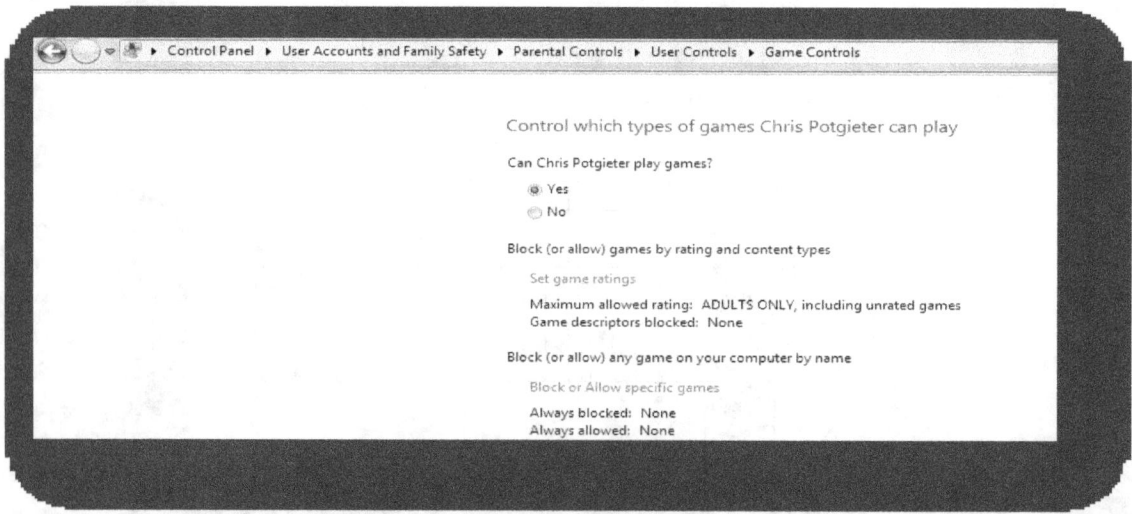

You can specify what rating games the user is allowed to access

You must specify the rating your child is allowed to access by clicking inside the little round circle next to the desired option. In our example Chris Potgieter is a 10 year old boy and therefor the option [everyone] is selected, since these programs/games are suitable for persons ages 6 and older and have minimum violence in these games and hopefully suitable language. Thus the child will not be allowed to access mature or adult content.

It is advisable to block games with no rating, since you will have no knowledge what the content of these games are and thus could affect your child in a negative way. Many games are available that states what their ratings are, it is much safer to use these games.

Block games with no ratings, by clicking inside the little round circle next to the option <Block games with no rating>

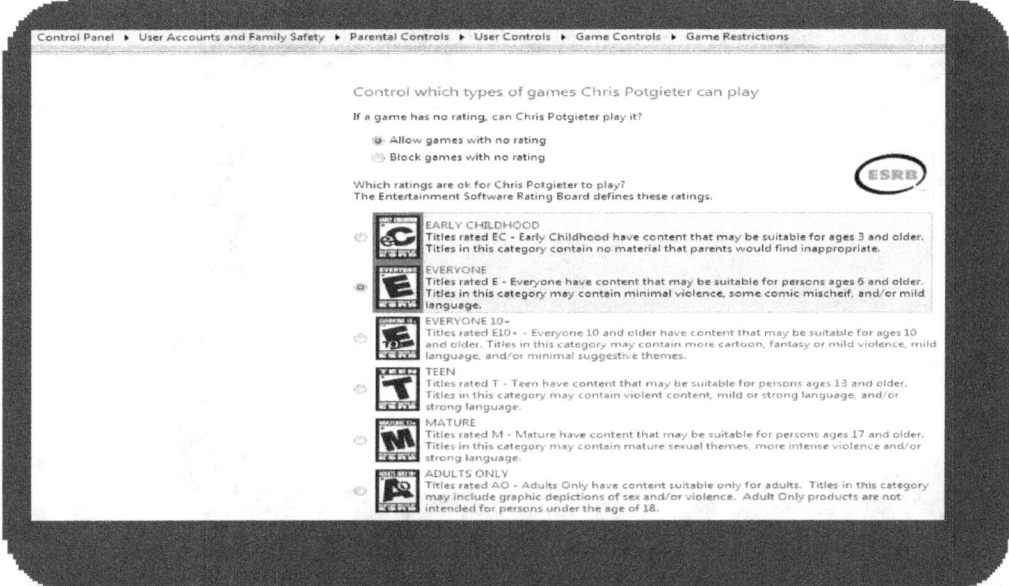

You can choose which games the user may play
Click inside the radio button (the little round circle) to choose an option
- If this user is not allowed to play the game, click on <always block>
- If the user is allowed to play the game, Click on <always allow>

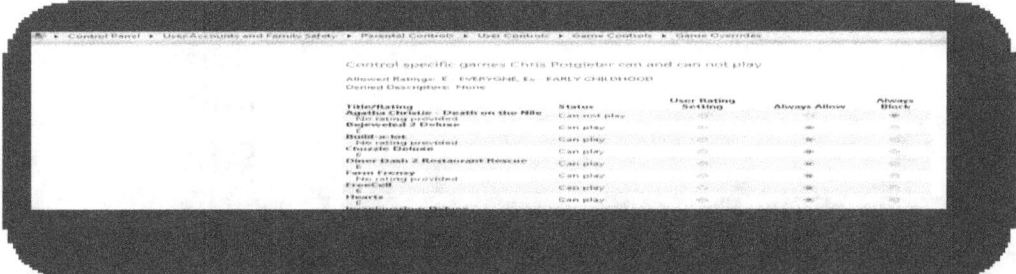

After you have implemented parental control, the options you've chosen will be listed on the account:

Like in the examples below:

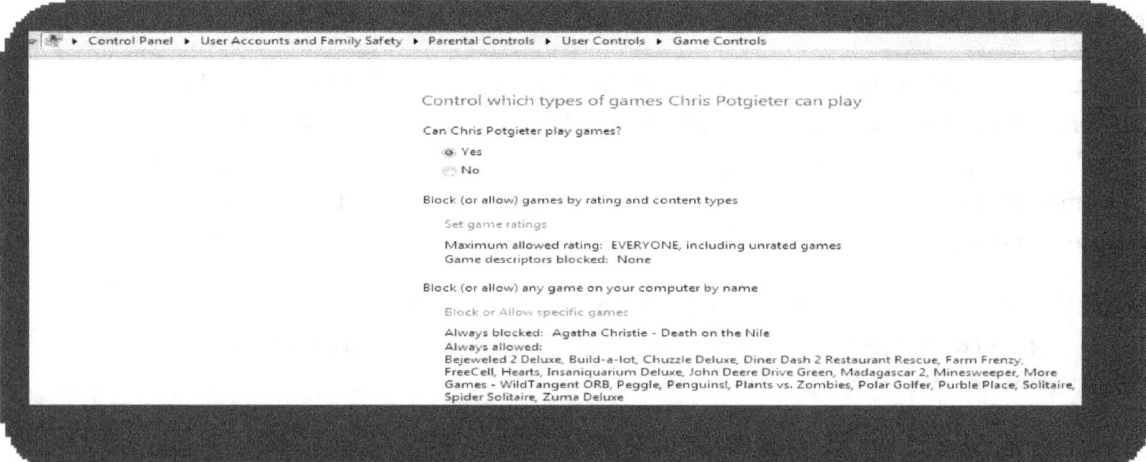

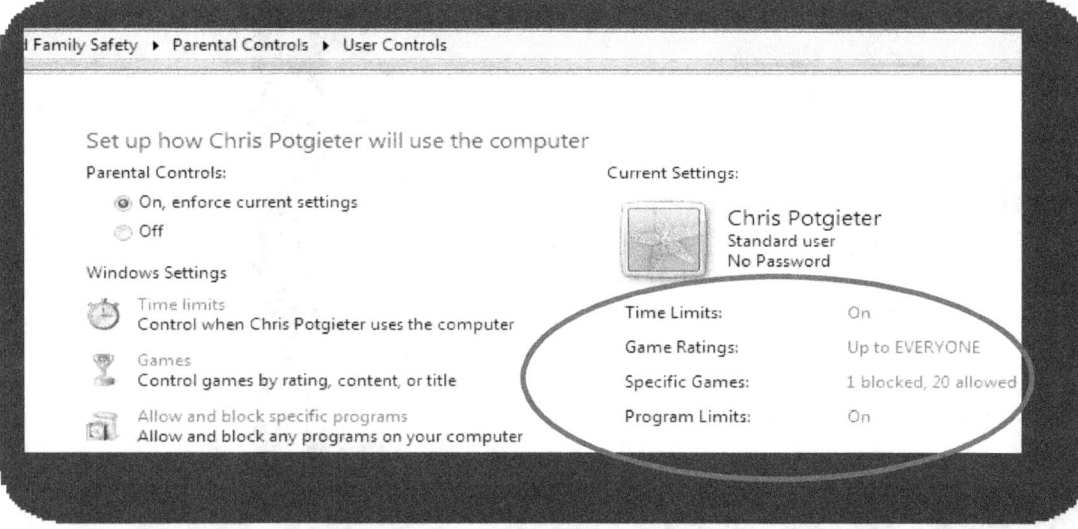

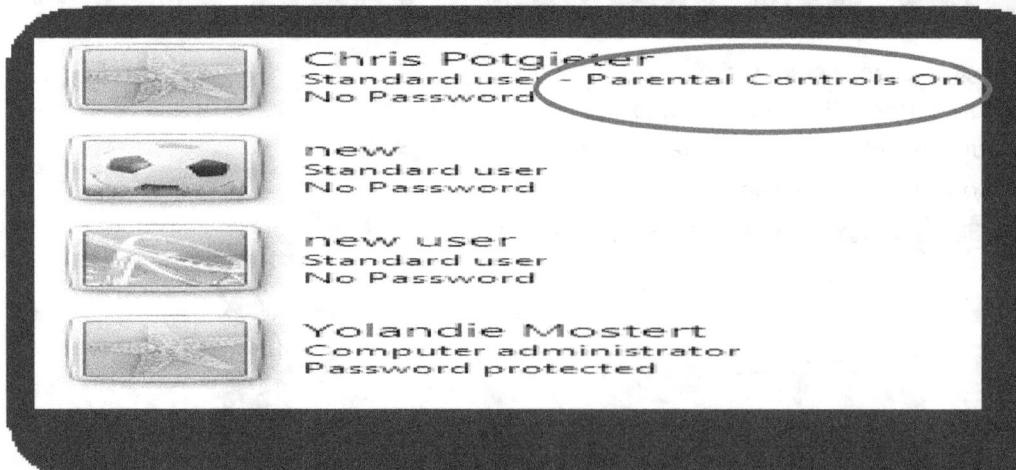

Troubleshooting your computer

If your screen freezes, meaning nothing happens when you press buttons, use the task manager instead of resetting the computer

How to activate the task manager:

Press <CTRL> <ALT><DELETE>

First press ctrl, don't release the button, now press alt, both buttons is now pressed in and don't release them, now press delete, all three buttons are pressed in to reveal the <Task Manager>

➢ Click on the option: <Start Task Manager>

The following screen will appear:

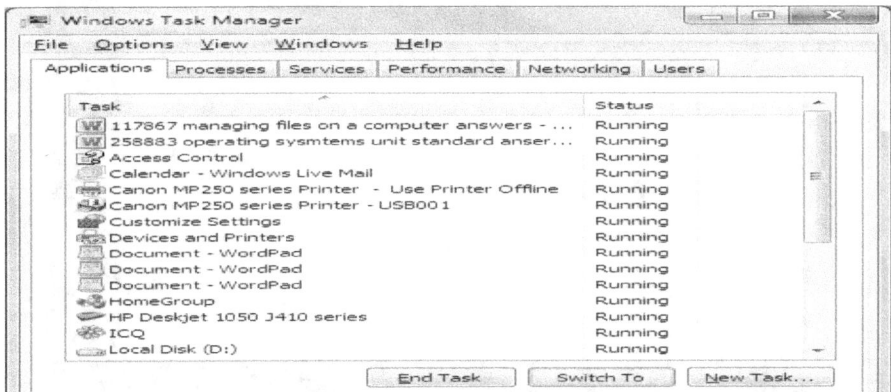

This is a list of all the programs that are currently in the computer's memory,

Look at the *status*, perhaps one of the programs will list that it is <not responding>

➢ Click on the program that is not responding
➢ Click on <end task>, if that doesn't work
➢ Click on <switch to>, and select another program to become active

If the computer is still not working, then and only then you may switch of the computer at the switch. *(There is always a 10% chance that the system files can get damaged when you don't use the shut down feature to shut down the computer)*

Restart the computer to see if it works, if it doesn't work. Use your backup disks to restore your computer to a working condition. Unless it's a hardware problem, usually re-installing windows will solve the problem.

Sometimes, not often, there is a conflict in resources or your computer runs out of memory, and then it helps to restart your computer, to clear resources and clear the memory. If this does not solve the problem, it is possible that you have accidently deleted a system file. If some of the system files have been deleted, you can simply re-install the system files.

Speech recognition

Microsoft speech recognition will type in any words you say into a document.

IT also allow you to command menus and open and close files with your voice.

Click on start, control panel, ease of access, speech recognition.

However my personal opinion is that windows speech recognition acts just like an average husband, it listen to half the things you say and the other half of the time it doesn't understand you and don't really do what you say unless you say it out loud and clear, If you don't give the instructions loud and clear, it will do whatever it thinks you want to get done and get it all wrong, or maybe it will do nothing.

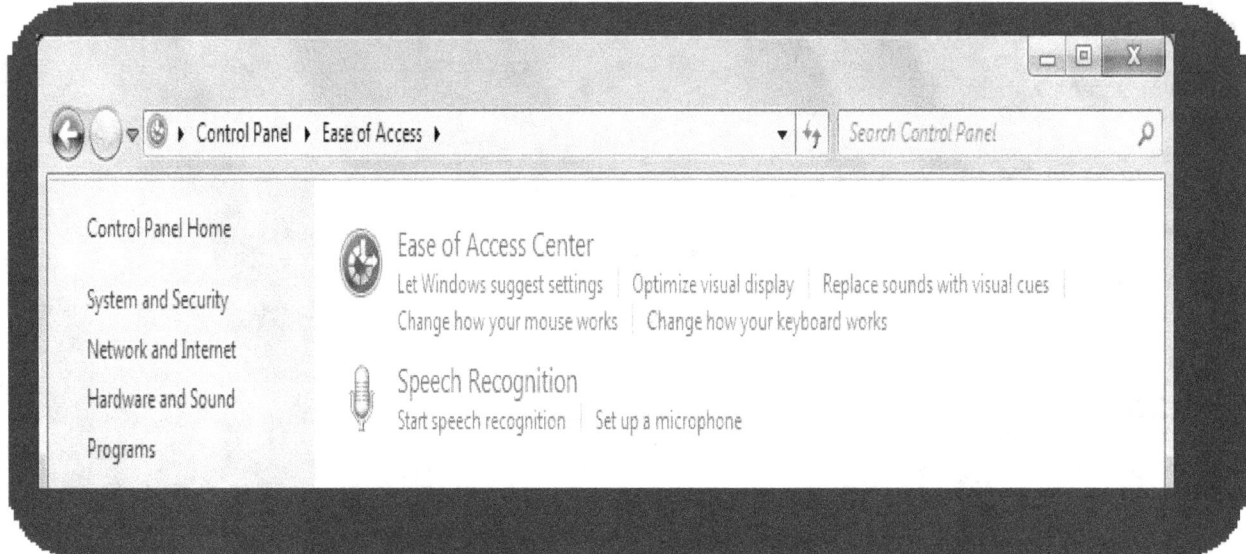

The programme works better after you have trained it to listen to your voice

- Click on<train your computer> if you wish to train the computer to listen to your commands
- Click on <start speech recognition> if you want to activate speech recognition

Click on the round circle to switch it off or on

Be careful the computer will pick up the slightest sound, and if you have a cold and sniff it might even type in the letter "S"

When you click on <speech recognition>, the following screen will appear:

When voice recognition is switched on say the following
"what can I say."
Windows will then provide the following dialog box, where you can choose which options to use
> ➢ Say "common speech recognition commands" a list of common commands will be listed
> ➢ Say" scroll down" say scroll up, you will scroll up and down the menu to select your options

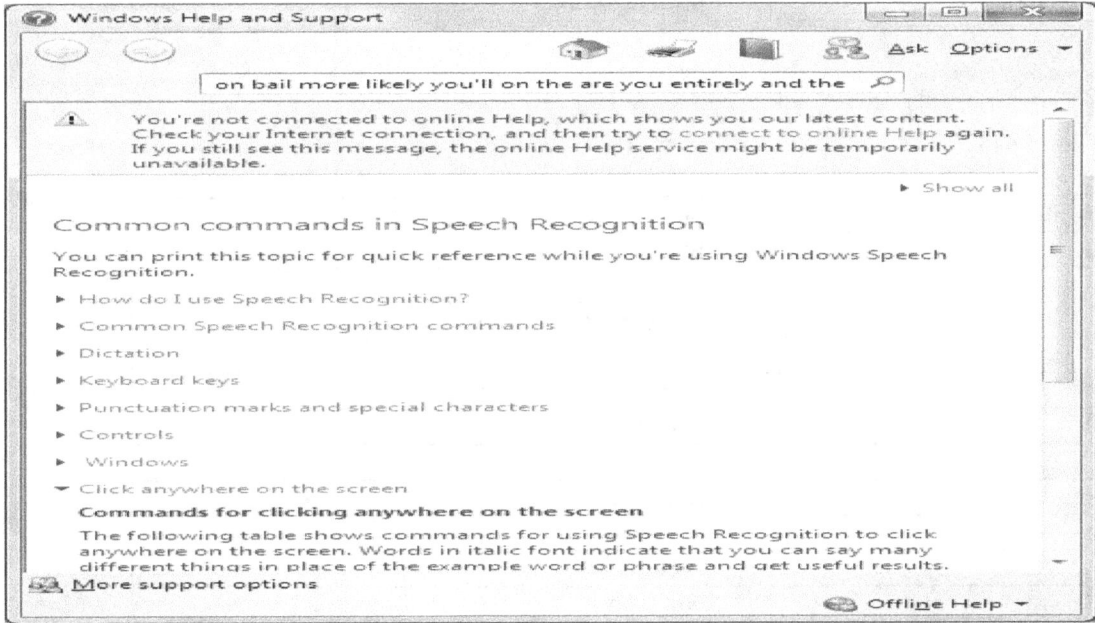

To activate options on the start menu

Action: This is what will happen	Speak: This is what you must say
Turn speech recognition on	Start listening
Switch to desktop	Switch to desktop
Activate the start menu	Start
Open notepad	Notepad
Using help	Help
Open ms excel	Microsoft excel
Open ms word	Microsoft word

When there is more than one option for windows to choose from, it will list numbers on the screen, and then you must say the number to select the item of your choice.

Activating desktop options

To cancel the start menu	Cancel
Go to desktop	Switch to desktop
select notepad from desktop	Notepad
Open note pad	Double click
Close notepad	Close that
Canceling an option	Cancel

Activating menus inside a program

Select the file menu	Click file
Select the save command	Save
Select the home tab	Click home
Stop the speech function	Stop listening

Typing a letter in word pad

Start speech recognition	Start listening
Select start menu	Start
Open wordpad	Wordpad
Type letters	Press Y press o press l
Type a word	Yolandie
Type a sentence	Yolandie is a my trainer and
Select a word	Select <and>
Delete a word	Delete
Delete a character	Backspace
Create a new line	New line
Period	Period
Full stop	Full stop

Moving the mouse
Say "Mouse grid" say "number" , say "click"

Selecting items with the mouse
Say " mouse grid" a list of numbers will appear
Say the number closest to the area you wish to select.
Say " mark"
Say the number where the mouse cursor must be dragged to, say click

Revision Exercises:

Do as many exercises as you want or follow the instructions of your trainer

Practise exercise: Windows

Open Windows Explorer

Maximize. Minimize and Close the Window

Practise exercise: creating folders

Create the following folder structure

C:\manuals\ word\level 1,2

C:\manuals\excel\level 1,2

C:\manuals\ windows 7

C:\manuals\ powerpoint

C:\manuals\ internet

Practise exercise Create a new user account with your name

> ➢ You are a standard user
> ➢ Allocate time between 5 am and 11 pm
> ➢ Allocate which programs you are allowed to use

Practise exercise Speech recognition

> ➢ Tell the computer to open windows explorer
> ➢ Tell the computer to close windows explorer

The following Utility functions are explained in book 2: **Windows 7 Utilities**

Please go here: www.QualityTraining.Yolasite.com to order digital copies in PDF format

Goto www.lulu.com/spotlight/worldpeace734 to get book 2 of windows 7 that include the following:

Utility programs
- Calculator
- Paint
- Wordpad and printing
- Notepad
- Windows fax and scan
- Windows live moviemaker
- Media player(to play music)
- Windows photogalery
- Windows live mail
- PDF and XPS reader
- MSN Windows Live Messenger(chatting online on internet)

If you are new to the computer environment it is also recommended that you also get the Internet Training manual, also located at www.lulu.com/spotlight/worldpeace734
You can also order more books at Quality1training@gmail.com

Some of the funds from these books will be used to help, educate poor people and animals and orphan boy, Thank you so much for all your support!!

Sincerely

Yolandie

www.ingramcontent.com/pod-product-compliance
Lightning Source LLC
Chambersburg PA
CBHW080825170526

45158CB00009B/2523